COVERING THE NEW YORKER

Feb. 26 & Mar. 4, 1996

THE NEW YORKER

Price $3.50

EUSTACIA TILLEY by R.O. Blechman
February 26 & March 4, 1996

COVERING THE NEW YORKER

CUTTING-EDGE COVERS FROM A LITERARY INSTITUTION

FRANÇOISE MOULY
Conversation with LAWRENCE WESCHLER

THE NEW YORKER ABBEVILLE PRESS PUBLISHERS
New York London Paris

This book is dedicated to my husband, Art Spiegelman, whose genius has been my most profound inspiration, and who, as quite a few other artists have remarked, has trained me well in the delicate art of dealing with artists on a daily basis. The thought of my children, Dashiell and Nadja, has given me courage through seemingly endless nights and weekends of work, while their kindness and wisdom have been my reward when I finally came home.

ACKNOWLEDGMENTS

I am deeply grateful to the team of extraordinary professionals put together by Greg Captain, of The New Yorker's Imaging Department, which produced the digital scans for this book, and to Anthony Bellacicco. Working with craftsmen of such talent and dedication is a rare privilege. Janice Yu worked on every stage of the book, and her intelligence and grace under pressure can never be adequately praised. I want to thank Eric Rayman, who convinced me that I could do this and proceeded to prove himself right. I am indebted to Chip Kidd for his advice on the cover, to Hannah Selinger and the many interns for their help, and to Paul Leopold for the entry from the Encyclopedia Britannica, which appears on page 6.

I would also like to thank the two editors under whom I've worked at The New Yorker, Tina Brown and David Remnick, who have consistently provided direction and motivation for the artists and for me. I am grateful to Pamela McCarthy for her valuable suggestions and for rallying the talents of Peter Canby, Edward Klaris, Anne Mortimer-Maddox, Kilian Schalk, Laura Stickney, Bill Wasik, and others behind this project. Ann Goldstein deserves special thanks for generously providing invaluable help with the text.

Finally, I would like to thank the people at Abbeville Press for their cooperative spirit, especially Mark Magowan, who believed in this book from the beginning, and Nancy Grubb, my editor, who took on the daunting task of organizing the text and was uncompromising in her belief of how good the project could be.

Last, I want to thank Lawrence Weschler, who lent the book much of his precious time. I am grateful to have had the support of someone whose appreciation of artists and their work runs so deep, and who can articulate so precisely that he makes you want to look at each picture again and again.

Edited and designed by FRANÇOISE MOULY
Cover and jacket design by FRANÇOISE MOULY

back cover, clockwise from top left:

EUSTACIA TILLEY by R.O. Blechman
February 26 & March 4, 1996

TILLEY by Art Spiegelman
published in the February 22, 1993, issue

ELVIS TILLEY by R. Crumb
February 21, 1994

FEBRUARY 21, 1925 by Rea Irvin

TILLEY by Charles Burns
published in the February 22, 1993, issue

FEBRUARY 21 & 28, 2000 by William Wegman

THE NEW YORKER REPACKAGED by Roz Chast
published in the February 22, 1993, issue

Library of Congress Cataloging-in-Publication Data

Mouly, Françoise
Covering The New Yorker: cutting-edge covers from a literary institution/Françoise Mouly with Lawrence Weschler.
p. cm.
Includes index.
ISBN 0-79892-0657-9 (alk.paper)
1. New Yorker (New York, N.Y.: 1925) 2. Magazine covers–New York (State)–New York. I. Weschler, Lawrence. II. New Yorker (New York, NY.: 1925) III. Title.

NC974.4.N48 M68 2000
741.6'52'0973–dc21 00-56550

ABBEVILLE PRESS
EDITOR: Nancy Grubb
ART DIRECTOR: Patricia Fabricant
PRODUCTION EDITOR: Max Dickstein
PRODUCTION MANAGER: Louise Kurtz

First edition

10 9 8 7 6 5 4 3 2 1

CONTENTS

INTRODUCTION

by Françoise Mouly

From *Fraser's Magazine*, Dec. 1834.
FIG. 47.—Count D'Orsay. Dress of a man of Fashion in Early Victorian Period.

top to bottom:
From the Encyclopedia Britannica
DECEMBER 28, 1929 *by Peter Arno*
MARCH 11, 1939 *by Constantin Alajálov*

You can't judge a book by its cover, but a magazine isn't so lucky—its personality is defined by its cover, and the rest of the magazine has to stand behind it. When I became art editor of *The New Yorker*, in 1993, I turned to the thirty-five hundred covers that had been published since the magazine began. The basic design, a full-bleed image with a narrow vertical strip of color on the left (known in-house as the "strap"), was established by the magazine's first art director, Rea Irvin. His cover for the first issue, February 21, 1925, so effectively established *The New Yorker's* sophisticated tone that it was published, nearly unchanged, every February until 1994. It depicts a stuffed shirt, later dubbed Eustace Tilley, raising his monocle to examine a butterfly. Irvin appears to have done what artists often do: he looked up references, including the image of an effete-looking dandy of 1834, dressed in the height of early Victorian fashion, reproduced in the costume section of the eleventh edition of the *Encyclopedia Britannica*. It seems likely that the target of Irvin's irony was the fossilized upper crust of New York society, a choice that clearly delighted the new, jazzy cultural élite. But Irvin's cover was also self-mocking.

Harold Ross, the founder of *The New Yorker*, was a Westerner who wanted to cover the glamorous life of New York in the Jazz Age. He modelled *The New Yorker* on the thriving humor magazines of the time, such as *Judge*, where he had been an editor. Ross assembled some of the best wits of a cynical generation bent on partying. Dorothy Parker, Robert Benchley, Alexander Woollcott, Franklin P. Adams, and others became known collectively as the Algonquin Round Table. The covers Ross published during the first few years featured bold graphics rendered in a limited palette of flat colors—often silhouetted figures against a one-dimensional background. Striking examples of the Art Deco style prevalent at the time, these covers were designed to function like posters; their concision and abstraction made the images instantly clear.

Soon, the high-society types who had first appeared as flat decorative design elements were rounded out both visually and narratively. With the addition of specific details and facial expressions, they became characters in storytelling images by such artists as Peter Arno, Will Cotton, Helen E. Hokinson, and Mary Petty. For example, the December 28, 1929, cover, by Arno, depicts a cluster of night-club revellers (a typical motif of the early covers), but here the central couple look uncomfortable and slightly embarrassed by their drunken neighbors. Although by the nineteen-thirties the party was over, *New Yorker* covers of the time rarely acknowledged the hardships of the Depression. Indeed, a March 11, 1939, cover by Constantin Alajálov shows a hesitant street peddler offering his goods to the disdainful passengers in the back of a chauffeured car.

By the end of the Second World War, *The New Yorker's* war reporting—culminating with John Hersey's August 31, 1946, report on Hiroshima—had established the magazine as more than a gathering of wits; it had become a preëminent voice in serious American

FEBRUARY 21, 1925
by Rea Irvin

journalism. But the cover of the famous "Hiroshima" issue did not portray Japanese children in flames; instead, it was a decorative tableau of New England vacationers, by Charles E. Martin. William Shawn, the managing editor, who had persuaded Ross to devote the entire issue to Hersey's report, may have had a say in the issue's cover as well. Certainly after he succeeded Ross as editor, in 1952, he brought about a major shift in the tenor of the covers; Shawn had his own vision for the magazine. In 1983, in response to queries from an ad salesman, he summed up his philosophy regarding the covers:

> *We have fewer covers today that have humor than we did years ago. They tend to be more aesthetic and the subject matter for the most part is New York City or the country around New York City. The suburbs, the countryside. Sometimes it's just a still-life of flowers or a plant. It's not supposed to be spectacular. When it appears on a newsstand, it's not supposed to stand out. It's a restful change from all the other covers, I'd say.*

Shawn's covers moved away from anecdotal storytelling; rather than depicting the foibles of the upper middle class, they reflected its aesthetic aspirations. More often than not, they presented landscapes and cityscapes in domesticated versions of Post-Impressionist painting styles, owing much to Picasso, Matisse, and Paul Klee. These aestheticized images, however, were overshadowed by the work of Shawn's most important discovery, Saul Steinberg. A witty visual philosopher of line and symbol, Steinberg expanded the vocabulary of modernism while acerbically commenting on the American scene. In 1985, S. I. Newhouse, Jr., the chairman of Condé Nast, acquired *The New Yorker*, and two years later Robert Gottlieb became the magazine's third editor. Gottlieb preserved Shawn's approach to cover art while adding Surrealist-derived imagery to the visual mix. By the time Tina Brown became the editor, in 1992, some critics saw the magazine as the embodiment of Eustace Tilley, the puffed-up dandy Irvin had once mocked.

When Brown was appointed editor, she decided on three artists she wanted to bring to the magazine: Richard Avedon (who became the first *New Yorker* staff photographer), Edward Sorel, and Art Spiegelman. The change in the magazine's attitude toward its times was heralded in her first cover, published on October 5, 1992: a drawing by Sorel of a leather-clad punk in a horse-drawn carriage in Central Park (page 35). That image gave notice that the self-satisfied dandy would have to contend with a new generation of cultural movers and shakers.

The cover that fully delivered on the threat was Spiegelman's 1993 Valentine's Day cover (page 103), showing a black woman and a Hasidic Jew in a loving embrace. At the time, the papers were filled with the bitter struggle between the black and Hasidic communities of Brooklyn's Crown Heights neighborhood. The cover was discussed and sometimes denounced in the media. Quite a few irate readers threatened to cancel their subscriptions, and there were heated arguments at dinner parties all over town (as there had been within the editorial offices of *The New Yorker*). The magazine, once polite, genteel, and retiring, had become the center of controversy. In Spiegelman's multilayered, irreverent, and ironic cover, Brown had found an image that provided a crucial component of the tone she wanted for the magazine.

top to bottom:
AUGUST 31, 1946 *by Charles E. Martin, for the "Hiroshima" issue*
JANUARY 22, 1972 *by Charles E. Martin*
JANUARY 6, 1992 *by Gürbüz Doğan Ekşioğlu*

Kiss has mouths agape

The ASSOCIATED PRESS

The New Yorker magazine was the talk of Crown Heights yesterday.

The cover of the magazine, which hit newsstands yesterday, shows a painting of a black woman and a Hasidic man embracing and kissing. It drew criticism from leaders on both sides of the racially troubled community.

But the artist, Pulitzer Prize winner Art Spiegelman, and the editor, Tina Brown, both said the Valentine's Day cover was a wishful advocacy of replacing conflict with love.

Spiegelman, in an accompanying commentary, acknowledged that his image is a dream that is "knowingly naive" and that the problems besetting the Jews and blacks of Crown Heights "cannot be kissed away."

"But once a year, perhaps, it's permissible, even if just for a moment, to close one's eyes, see beyond the tragic complexities of modern life, and imagine that it might really be true that 'All you need is love.'"

The artist won a special Pulitzer last year for "Maus: A Survivor's Tale," a two-volume comic book about the Nazi Holocaust.

"I think that instead of healing anything, there will be anger emanating because of this," said the Rev. Herbert Daughtry, an activist black minister.

Daughtry and Rabbi Joseph Spielman, chairman of the Crown Heights Jewish Community Council, both called the painting "unfortunate."

"Rather than healing, this just makes everything ludicrous," Spielman said, pointing out that Hasidim may not even kiss their wives or show them physical affection in public.

Daughtry also said he doubted that the magazine would have used a cover showing a black man kissing a Hasidic woman.

Spiegelman, speaking from Fort Lauderdale, said he had tried just such a version, "but a Hasidic woman is not iconically recognizable — just a woman in a kerchief."

"Even if that weren't a problem, then it would be, 'How dare you. You're showing a black man as a rapist,'" Spiegelman said.

The man in the painting is unmistakably a Hasid, bearded, side-curled and wearing a black hat and coat. The brown-skinned woman has her hair in dreadlocks.

The reaction made him sad, Spiegelman said, but, he added: "If it unites both communities against me, at least we've gotten them united."

NEW YORK DAILY NEWS, FEB. 9, 1993

It was shortly thereafter that she asked me to join the staff as art editor. I was startled. Together with Art Spiegelman (my husband), I had published and co-edited the magazine *RAW*, but *RAW* was distinctly downtown, an avant-garde magazine of comics and graphics, far from the world of *The New Yorker*. At first I was reluctant to give up the independence afforded by self-publishing, but Brown's idea of bringing radical change to a magazine with such a distinguished history presented an irresistible challenge. While reëngaging its subscribers, the magazine had to establish once again a strong presence on the newsstand so that new generations of readers might discover it.

It seemed to me that *New Yorker* covers in the postmodern nineties could reflect a broad spectrum of artistic idioms and styles. Rummaging through the magazine's history, I was attracted to the decorative qualities of the twenties covers; their posterlike immediacy provided an important object lesson in images that must catch your attention instantly on a crowded newsstand. The influences of the "high" arts evident in Shawn's covers offered a hint of how images could also stand up to scrutiny on more than half a million coffee tables. But it was the covers that told a story—like Will Cotton's exhausted 1936 matron pausing to rest while trekking through an art museum (page 185), and William Steig's Valentine's Day cover also from 1936 (page 102), showing a precocious schoolboy mooning over a curvaceous young woman—which offered the richest possibilities for a revitalized *New Yorker*. Such covers provided a snapshot of what urban sophisticates cared about, their attitudes and prejudices, their mannerisms and jokes. I've wanted to build a series of images that, looked at from a later vantage point, might create a portrait of our society.

New Yorker artists have an opportunity—indeed, a mandate—to express their point of view. *The New Yorker* is the only remaining wide-circulation publication that still relies on free-standing illustrated covers (other magazine covers are dictated by the need to illustrate the "cover story," usually with a photograph, and are cluttered with written blurbs). When an artist does a cover for us, it is a personal statement that represents his concept, his joke.

Saul Steinberg once said that there were certain pictures that would change the way a person saw the world, that the viewer wouldn't be able to erase from his memory. Such images are rare, but they're what we strive for. I find it essential to maintain a constant back-and-forth with a large group of artists. Some, like Edward Sorel, Jean-Jacques Sempé, Barry Blitt, and Art Spiegelman, are primarily cartoonists. Others, like Mark Ulriksen, Lorenzo Mattotti, and Anita Kunz, are primarily illustrators. Still others, like William Joyce and Maira Kalman, are children's-book authors. What all the artists have in common is that they know how to make a point succinctly and attractively.

Few artists are hit by inspiration until they make themselves focus on the task before them. Anita Kunz says that she sits down at her drawing table determined to come up with a certain number of sketches, treating the assignment as if it were a school project. To help get the artists going, I systematized *The New Yorker's* tradition of publishing seasonal

top to bottom:

Cover of RAW No. 1, by Art Spiegelman, 1980
Cover of RAW No. 3, by Gary Panter, 1981
Cover of "How to Commit Suicide in South Africa," by Sue Coe, 1983
All published by RAW Books & Graphics.

images, and I regularly send the artists a calendar of suggested topics. It includes the seasons; holidays such as Valentine's Day, Easter, and Mother's Day; and the themes of the magazine's recently introduced special issues. I supplement this list with conversations and E-mails suggesting events and subjects that might yield memorable pictures. It's only because we schedule a season's worth of covers in advance that we can, occasionally, turn around a cover on a hot topic in twenty-four or forty-eight hours.

New York City is a constant source of images that can run anytime, that are not tied to a particular event or time of year, such as Eric Drooker's businessmen on stilts, wobbly masters of the universe striding among the skyscrapers of the city (page 24), and Edward Sorel's depiction of barnyard animals in a double-decker tourist bus looking down at the exotic creatures of Gotham's streets (page 35). Leaving the city inspired Peter de Sève's memorable summer cover (page 156) of New Yorkers crowding New England harbors, which portrays the city dwellers as pigeons being looked down upon condescendingly by a blasé seagull.

Shifts in the culture are prime source material for the cover artists. Often, the reaction from readers is linked to their feelings about the phenomenon or trend portrayed. The artist is the messenger, sometimes hailed as a hero, sometimes pilloried. A 1994 June wedding cover by Jacques de Loustal (page 129) showed two men about to cut the wedding cake on a background of shocking pink. Many readers were angry, while many others called and asked for a print of the image they could frame. In June of 1996, an image by Barry Blitt (page 65) of two sailors kissing in Times Square, in a pose reminiscent of the well-known V-J Day photograph by Eisenstaedt, drew protests from the sailor who had supposedly been in the original photo as well as other Second World War veterans, while opponents of President Clinton's "Don't ask, don't tell" policy rallied behind it. A recent (May 15, 2000) Mother's Day cover, by Carter Goodrich, of a Mother Earth type and a skinny working woman sitting side by side on a bench (page 124) elicited the following range of responses: "Carter Goodrich is a genius." "I LOVE this cover of the fecund Mother Earth and the pale angular New York career girl looking on with disgust and desire." "A gross trivialization of motherhood." "Working women everywhere will feel uplifted by the message that their professional endeavors are nothing compared to the ability to reproduce." "Does the tortured expression on the face of the unhappy career girl signify aversion and disgust—or overwhelming longing for a child of her own?" "I'm surprised that so sophisticated a magazine would engage in such a stereotypical illustration." "Carter Goodrich's 'Mother Nature' is brilliant. It epitomizes the kind of social observation that *The New Yorker* considers its eminent domain."

It is a testament to the loyalty of longtime readers that their attachment to the magazine has survived the changes that have transformed *The New Yorker* over the last decade. Many readers had hoped we would provide a respite from the saturation of coverage surrounding the O. J. Simpson murder case, but they appreciated the many meanings of the comment on the affair by HA (Bob Zoell), published at the start of the trial (page 61). Zoell's simple still-life of orange juice on a white background showed a glass that is half full

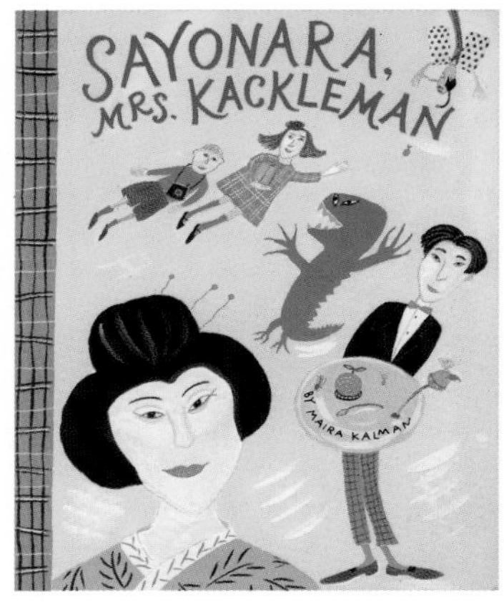

top to bottom:
"Doctor De Soto," by William Steig (Farrar, Straus & Giroux), 1982
"Dinosaur Bob," by William Joyce (HarperCollins), 1988
"Sayonara, Mrs. Kackleman," by Maira Kalman (Puffin Books), 1989

or half empty, depending on one's point of view. For knowledgeable readers, the image also evoked Shawn's still-life covers. It was a visual pun on orange juice and O.J.'s guilt or innocence, and it was a cover on a sensational topic that resembled the most adamantly nontopical covers.

Though *New Yorker* covers now often reflect current events, on rare occasions an image can actually affect those events. In February of 1999, an African immigrant, Amadou Diallo, was killed by New York City police in the vestibule of his apartment building. Apparently without provocation, Diallo was shot at forty-one times. The Police Department and the Mayor offered no explanation of why so many shots were fired, insisting that an investigation was under way. Then Art Spiegelman proposed an image (page 83) that expressed the outrage many New Yorkers felt: a sweet-looking old-fashioned cop at a Coney Island shooting gallery aims his semi-automatic at anonymous civilian targets. A sign on the stand reads: "41 shots—10¢."

Because of production logistics, David Remnick, who in 1998 became the magazine's fifth editor, had to be woken up at nearly midnight on a Thursday and was faxed an extremely rough sketch of the idea. He promptly gave his O.K., and the image was finished and transmitted digitally to the printer, in Kentucky, twenty-four hours later. On Monday, when the magazine reached the newsstands, the cover was denounced in press conferences by the Police Commissioner, the Mayor, and the Governor. The cover helped catalyze protests against the police. Local demonstrations broadened as movie stars and civil-rights activists joined picketers at Police Headquarters. Meanwhile, off-duty police officers staged a demonstration outside *The New Yorker's* offices to protest the cover. The image was cited by an appellate court as one of the reasons the trial of the police officers involved in Diallo's death had to be moved outside New York City.

Indeed, David Remnick has encouraged artists to deal with New York City not only as the figurative capital of world culture but also as a specific place. His background as a journalist has led him to seek out covers that focus on political issues as well as social ones. As someone who grew up reading *The New Yorker*, Remnick has taken advantage of the new paths opened by Tina Brown, while hoping to synthesize and preserve the magazine's traditions. A May 31, 1999, cover by Bruce McCall (page 19), painted in his deadpan retro style, conjures up Times Square—not the recently renovated crossroads of commerce, or the squalid Times Square of the postwar era, but a "Lost Times Square" that never was, showing top-hatted swells on a street filled with high-culture entertainment and highbrow signs, a street that Eustace Tilley would have been delighted to visit.

By going back to its beginnings, *The New Yorker* has been reborn and has even stimulated the renewed use of illustrations, drawings, and cartoons in other publications. This seventy-five-year-old institution's weekly visual offerings—sometimes explosive, never predictable, always noticed—are a testament to the power of drawing. The new *New Yorker* covers have become an important part of America's cultural dialogue. Demonstrating that printed pictures are far from obsolete, these drawings stand out in the wired world of transient and fleeting images. ●

top to bottom:
O.J. cover by HA (Bob Zoell)
SEPTEMBER 10, 1979 *by Pierre Le-Tan*
Computer rough sketch of Diallo cover by Art Spiegelman

COVERING THE NEW YORKER

A Conversation Between Françoise Mouly and Lawrence Weschler

top to bottom:
top: JUNE 16, 1962 *by Abe Birnbaum, for the first of three "Silent Spring" issues*
center: MARCH 2, 1963 *by Susanne Suba, for the third of five "Eichmann in Jerusalem" issues*
bottom: FEBRUARY 1, 1982 *by Roxie Munro, for the first of three "Fate of the Earth" issues*

LAWRENCE WESCHLER: People talk about the timelessness of early *New Yorker* covers, but there were occasions even then when *New Yorker* covers were right on the money in terms of catching the moment.

FRANÇOISE MOULY: That was certainly true at the beginning, under Harold Ross, the founder and first editor. The insistence on not doing anything connected to the moment started under William Shawn, who became editor in the nineteen-fifties, and that mind-set was totally locked in by the seventies.

LW: What's striking is that when you reviewed the previous thirty-five hundred issues of the magazine, you were drawn to Ross's *New Yorker*. You show an active interest in the covers of the first twenty or thirty years and less in the later ones.

FM: For me, that's partly because in Ross's magazine the artists and the writers were viewed as equally important. In Shawn's *New Yorker*, artists were considered an important component of the magazine, but in terms of intellectual vitality there was less back-and-forth, less cross-pollination, than there had been in Ross's magazine. Gradually, as the magazine's focus shifted, and it became less a humor magazine, the artists became somewhat marginalized.

LW: But isn't it the case that the cover of a Shawn *New Yorker* functioned as a kind of moral center of an idealized world at a time when the magazine's contents included all the things that were threats to that world, so that the quietness of the cover operated as an assertion in its own right? If there was a peaceful cover of a suburban lawn, inside the magazine there was, say, a review of Michael Harrington's "The Other America," and that cover said, "You know, it would be nice for everybody to have this kind of peacefulness, but let's not fool ourselves." It was a very layered cover, but it wasn't removed from the world, though on a different magazine it could have been. One could imagine a magazine with that cover that was completely oblivious of the world and that talked only about the comforts of life—say, *House & Garden*.

FM: I agree with you that a magazine's cover always posits the ideal world and the ideal reader and the ideal that the magazine itself aspires to, because magazines are all about aspirations. I also agree that it was a conscious decision on Shawn's part to divorce the cover from the contents. And I think he could do that because at the time the magazine was extremely successful and self-confident. It had an audience of readers who, in the privacy of their own homes, in their back yards, were taking the time to read an article about what was going on in the inner city. But at a certain point the dynamics of the magazine had to change.

LW: Granted, there's absolutely no way that the old, Shawnian covers would have been appropriate for the magazine under Tina Brown or the magazine thereafter. That's not a value judgment—it's just a fact. The challenge becomes to figure out a different way.

FM: Right, because the magazine itself had to adapt to its time and the cover had to reflect that.

LW: The role of the cover in Shawn's *New Yorker*, however, was different from its role in either Ross's or Tina's. The covers for the four issues in which Truman Capote's "In Cold Blood" ran, for example, seemed almost militantly not to have anything to do with what was inside the magazine. I would argue that precisely because the magazine was into such terrifying stuff—Rachel Carson's "Silent Spring," Jonathan Schell's "The Fate of the Earth," Hannah Arendt's "Eichmann in Jerusalem"—and expressed such moral seriousness, the cover functioned as a kind of *cordon sanitaire* between the world and the heavy stuff inside. In other words, you had quiet, pastoral covers about peace (in some kind of E. B. White-like way), about a fantasy of order and so on, which allowed the magazine behind that cover to have, say, the most vivid reporting on Vietnam of its time. Similarly, as long as you had a serious Notes and Comment at the beginning of The Talk of the Town, you could have Donald Barthelme and all kinds of other wacked-out stuff in the rest of the magazine. There was a kind of moral groundedness that allowed the funny stuff to get funnier and weirder.

FM: I think that's totally accurate, but that *cordon sanitaire* kept out the artists who were defining their time. In the late sixties and seventies, there was a visually engaged narrative going on in the underground press that was in direct contrast to *The New Yorker*. In fact, *The New Yorker* went so far in the other direction that it created a generation gap for the artists. There was also definitely a geographical shift in the focus of the contributors at that point; many didn't live in New York. They came in once a week and they submitted their drawings, but their thinking process was not engaged in the same way as when they had been part of the life of the city. They also were not engaged in the cultural dialogue that was taking place in other media. No artist was working both for *The New Yorker* and for the underground press. That wasn't even conceivable.

LW: Well, things have certainly changed in that regard. A remarkable amount of controversy has surrounded many of the more recent covers. I assume that was in part your intention.

FM: I think one of the reasons that people tend to feel alienated from the political process and from the media nowadays is a surfeit of images that are all equivalent. We have so many mass-produced, commercially oriented images, but very few individually produced images that come from a thinking brain and address a thinking reader. I think artists have the ability to capture certain moments and to enhance reality to a point where it becomes shared reality. The artist doesn't function in a vacuum. He doesn't create the feeling that is in the air, but he has a way of catalyzing it and forcing one's attention to it.

LW: The air is, as it were, heavy-laden, charged with potential. The artist serves as a sort of lightning strike—his intervention is almost literally electrifying—and I suppose it's no

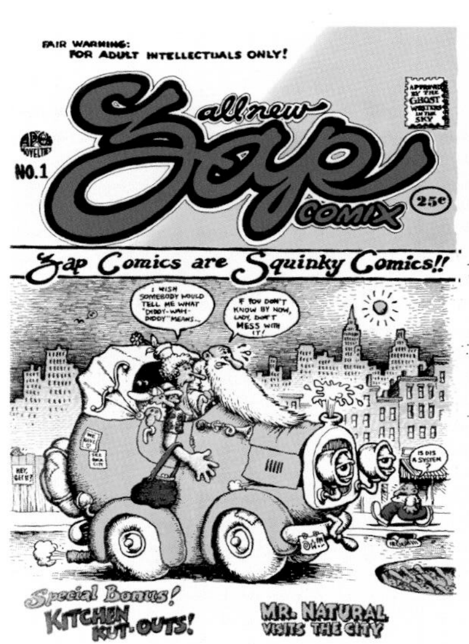

top to bottom:
April 2, 1969, cover of The East Village Other, by Art Spiegelman
1973 portrait of Nixon, by Edward Sorel
Zap Comix No. 1, by R. Crumb, 1967

wonder that some readers occasionally end up feeling singed. Of course, it's an old story.

FM: Precisely. What's interesting to me is to remember that there was a time, at the turn of the last century, when the illustrated press and its artists were not just decorators of other people's ideas; they were providing the cultural dialogue.

LW: Providing and provoking . . .

FM: The artists for those magazines were expressing strong convictions and delivering the message of the editorial staff—partly because good drawings are so efficient. Every revolution needs a poster artist. Radical humor magazines played a crucial role in European cultural and political life at that time. There was *Punch* in England, which had started in 1841, and the French humor sheets, such as *Le Rire* and *Le Chat Noir*, at the end of the nineteenth century. They, in turn, inspired the German *Simplicissimus*, which, though it began as a satirical journal, had its greatest impact through the work of its artists and cartoonists. *Simplicissimus* attacked the Kaiser, the government, the clergy. In the early years, its artists were jailed, and the magazine was censored and banned. In 1901, France saw the advent of an anti-establishment publication, *L'Assiette au Beurre*—a lavishly produced magazine devoted entirely to drawings. For artists at the turn of the century, politics was extremely important. They had to take a stand on their conception of art's role in society. Many of those involved with *L'Assiette au Beurre* made a commitment to art as political satire, to art for the masses. These European magazines were later the inspiration for *The Masses*, a left-wing magazine started here in 1911 that combined art and literature with a radical stance. I don't think, however, that such left-wing publications were the inspiration for Harold Ross. He was more influenced by the American magazines that had come out of the older *Punch* and *Le Rire*, as well as by *Judge* and *Life* (the humor magazine) here in the States.

top to bottom:

Drawing by Bruno Paul for Simplicissimus, Vol. VII, No. 46, 1902/3
Issue of L'Assiette au Beurre devoted to "Les Suicides," by Juan Gris, August 21, 1909
Page from L'Assiette au Beurre, by Jean Veber

LW: What influenced you?

FM: My entire generation in France came of age with *Hara-Kiri Hebdo*, an anarcho-left-wing weekly humor magazine. What everyone would rush to see in it—and all that anyone remembers now—is the work of the cartoonists. For me, it's an inspiration to know that there have been all these different publications in which artists have played a central role in shaping the world around them. I started out in this field by learning to operate my own printing press and running off artists' pamphlets. I have immense respect and appreciation for artists such as Saul Steinberg, who have consistently turned away from the lure of the world of fine art, and the fossilization of the creative process that can go on there, because they believe in the power of the printed page and because they want their work in the hands of many, many readers rather than exclusively on the walls of the very, very few.

LW: Do you give artists ideas for their covers?

FM: In editorial meetings, there are times when someone will say, for instance, "We should have an image about roller blades." And then somebody will exclaim, "Oh, that's a great idea," and I can't help it, I have to say, "Sorry, that's not an idea, that's a topic." It's a beginning of something, but an image will exist only when an artist comes up with an idea about that topic that makes it resonant.

LW: Visual storytelling, or visual narrative, is about staging, about getting the right order, just the way a good storyteller has to tell it in the right order.

FM: Timing and staging are everything. I remember a back-and-forth with Peter de Sève, which led to "Tailed" (page 95). At the time, women who wore fur coats were being attacked by animal-rights advocates. That was definitely a good topic to address, and it came up in my conversations with Peter about possible winter covers. He faxed a rough sketch of a bunch of animals lying in wait on a street corner; on the other side of the page a woman wearing a fur coat is walking her dog. It was good, it was funny, but the composition was too much like a split screen: you saw her, you saw them, but you never quite got to that moment of meeting. I told Peter, "I think you have something there," and asked him to keep going.

Peter has done a lot of work in animation, and you can see that he's very good at funny-animal cartoons. He also had this Upper East Side woman, a Hokinson lady, the perfect character to be wearing a fur coat. The Hokinson lady, as defined by Helen E. Hokinson in countless *New Yorker* cartoons and covers of the nineteen-thirties (see page 102), has been a rich source of inspiration for several of our contemporary artists. At any rate, Peter's main characters were right; now it was a matter of staging the idea correctly. He quickly moved into this new image, which has the woman, alone on a deserted sidewalk by Central Park, seeing an animal behind her (without turning her head—one of the conventions of cartooning). Out of all the animals in his first sketch he selected the bear, and then the raccoon, which, because it has a bandit mask, can be menacing and cute at the same time. De Sève played with the scale of this rather large lady followed by this tiny raccoon, which is nonetheless very full of itself. And then he set up another tiny animal ahead of her, her nervous little pet, and balanced her in the ambiguity between animal and animal. And it's perfect. It's absolutely Peter's idea and fully his realization, but I feel that our dialogue was useful in encouraging him and in refining the concept. That's what I mean when I say that, in my own way, I try to do for artists what I imagine *The New Yorker* under Shawn did for writers.

LW: How else do you try to intervene in the artistic process?

FM: An image has to work on many different levels, and it has to read instantly to make its point. A lot of my dialogue with the artists centers on that. If I were to tell an artist, I think it would be better if you did this in blue rather than in red, because that's my aesthetic judgment, I'd get nowhere, because it would just be my aesthetic judgment versus his. So instead I'll say, Well, I left your sketch on the wall and nobody got it, or they got it after two and a half seconds, therefore you need to address this. That's not an exaggeration. I put a cover sketch on the wall and I watch people look at it, and I time the laugh, or the "Hmm," or the "Wow!" Often I do this when other artists come to my office. And when I hear that "Wow!" I know they're furious because they've seen something that's really good and it's making them jealous. But when they go "Hmm, well," and they're tilting their heads from one side to the

top to bottom:
Three stages in the development of "Tailed," January 24, 1994, by Peter de Sève

other and they're spending a long time with it, then I know that the image still needs fine-tuning.

LW: Do you have favorite images among all the ones you've worked on?

FM: My honest answer is that what I like is the fact that one week we are running a cover by R. Crumb and the next week a cover by Saul Steinberg and the week after that a cover by Bruce McCall and on and on. What I take pride in is being able to have access to all those artists and to juxtapose their work and to be at a magazine that's broad enough to encompass them all. There's no longer a house look at *The New Yorker.* It's something I certainly tried to avoid when I did my own magazine, *RAW.* There we tried to bring together as many different styles, as many different artists, and as many different sensibilities as possible, and I think that's also one of the strengths of *The New Yorker.* Each writer has his voice, and it's the overall quality that distinguishes a *New Yorker* piece. In the same way, it's the quality of the visual comment that makes a cover feel like a *New Yorker* cover, the fact that it actually has something to say and says it so well.

LW: Your job reminds me of a scene in the film "Jonah Who Will Be 25 in the Year 2000." The old locomotive engineer says, "Well, it's one thing to be in a train as a passenger and see the world passing by." In a certain sense your knowing the thirty-five hundred covers, and seeing the past eight years of covers, which are spread out along the walls outside your office, can be compared to the view out the window of that train, and the rest of us, getting the magazine every week, have pretty much the same view. The engineer, however, continues, "But it's completely different to be in the front, where the world is coming at you and you are going into the world." It seems to me, sitting here in this office, that it's almost as if we were in the engineer's cab, or some kind of cockpit, with that fax machine giving you advance warning of things coming at you. You have the whole train of knowledge, the history of *The New Yorker,* the history of *L'Assiette au Beurre,* the history of *Simplicissimus,* of the Ross *New Yorker,* the Shawn *New Yorker.* And then coming out of that fax machine are the ideas that are plunging you into the up-to-date and even before the up-to-date. It's an interesting place to be.

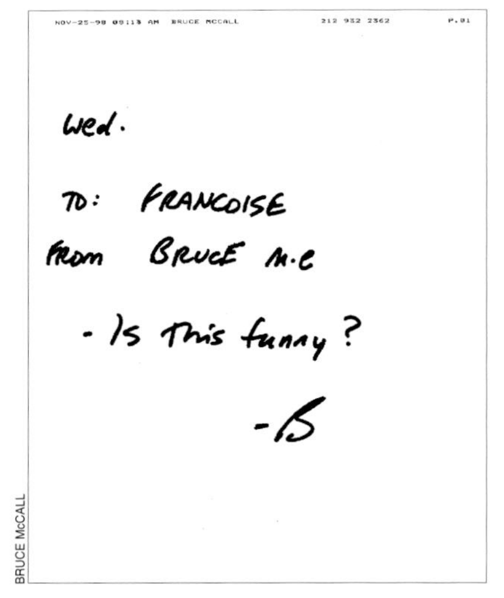

BRUCE McCALL

MARK ULRIKSEN

FM: It really is. I feel privileged and I'm especially grateful to the artists who have hung in there against all the odds. The rewards are so paltry and the venues so few for somebody who is able to draw and who is able to think, for an artist who can come up with something interesting and funny, for an artist who is engaging with his times. I'm grateful to all the artists who are still artists in this day and age and haven't become scriptwriters for Hollywood (though quite a few of the artists do that as well). Still, the core of their work, their true inspiration, the source of their thinking process and their creative life is drawing.

LW: And drawing is a wonderful word: drawing on, drawing from, being drawn to . . .

FM: And I'm also grateful to *The New Yorker,* because the immense respect accorded to the magazine—the poetry, the cartoons, the fiction, the reporting pieces, the critics, The Talk of the Town—works to give credibility and added import to the artists' statements. Putting drawings on the cover of *The New Yorker* keeps artists at the center of the cultural dialogue, and I can't think of a better place for them to be. ●

FEBRUARY 21 & 28, 2000
by William Wegman

THE BIG CITY

SEPTEMBER 22, 1928
by Adolph K. Kronengold

opposite:
LOST TIMES SQUARE by Bruce McCall
May 31, 1999

IN AT HOME TO BE A
CURATOR
JU-66060
ESCAR TO GO
ET TU, BUD
LEARN LATIN
CALL MCXMV
HARP CITY
PERA
25 DANCERS
24 NO COVER
1000'S OF ADULT LIBRETTOS
FRENCH HORNS
tatouille SHACK
FREE LIBRARY
ITALIAN MARBLE
SHAKESPEARE THEATRE
TREASURES OF GEOLOGY
RENOIR
POETRY
ROLLS ROY
BALLET R
World's Hottest Harpsichordist!!
Wanda LANDOWSKA
CUMMERBUNDS
Fabergé
G.B.SHAW TONITE
COGNAC
GREEK
TRAGI-THO
DITHYRAM
ALL-ST
"Silk Dressing Gowns? Dear Boy! WILBERFORCE of course!"
-Noël Coward
LONDON - PARIS
LILY PONS
"What A Set Of Pipes!"
- TOSCANINI
MIME Studio
MURNAU
DUTCH DOCUMENTARY FESTIVAL
FRESH FOIE GRAS
BRUCE McCALL

L·DOVE

opposite:
JULY 20, 1929
by Leonard Dove

JULY 3, 1954
by Charles E. Martin

Whenever possible, new artists spend time in The New Yorker library, looking at the old covers (which often seem very modern). Sometimes old covers are direct inspirations for new ones, and sometimes, as with Juliette Borda's image here, the result is a good mixture of the traditional New Yorker cover with a contemporary style.

left:

MARCH 3, 1962
by Arthur Getz

below, left:

WINDOW BOX
by Juliette Borda
September 7, 1998

below, right:

OCTOBER 26, 1929
by Theodore G. Haupt

opposite:

Eric Drooker is primarily an artist rather than an illustrator. Although his images are realistically rendered, his visions of individuals in the city are dreamlike as well as iconic.

UPWARDLY MOBILE by Eric Drooker
September 30, 1996

LIFE AT THE TOP by Eric Drooker
September 12, 1994

WATER AND FIRE by Eric Drooker
March 20, 1995

left:

MAY 6, 1944
by Peter Arno

far left:

SOMETHING IN THE AIR
by Ian Falconer
September 16, 1996

below, left:

SOMETHING FOR EVERYONE
by Roz Chast
November 22, 1999

Roz Chast is essential to the contemporary New Yorker, in part because she has the ability to exaggerate just slightly what is all around us. Here she is commenting on the specialization of magazines, and it's particularly ironic that she does so on the cover of a magazine that is one of the few remaining that are not specialized.

below, right:

APRIL 22, 1939
by Leonard Dove

opposite:

HELTER SWELTER
by Michael Roberts
August 5, 1996

M.R.

MAY 10, 1930
by Theodore G. Haupt

CITY IN MOURNING by Ana Juan
August 2, 1999
This cover ran the week after John F. Kennedy, Jr., died in a plane crash, with his wife and her sister.

left:
October 5, 1957
by Arthur Getz

below, left:
Disturbing the Peace
by Ian Falconer
January 20, 1997

below, right:
April 2, 1927
by San Toyo

opposite:
At the End of the Tunnel
by Eric Drooker
September 18, 1995

DROOKER

CITY OF DREAMS
by Edward Sorel
February 22 & March 1, 1999

THE ROAR OF THE CROWD
by Edward Sorel
May 22, 1995

EDWARD SOREL

As a young man, Sorel wanted to do cartoons and covers for *The New Yorker*, but he wasn't accepted into what was then, by and large, a closed shop. It is poetic justice that he has since become one of the magazine's star artists. He knows intuitively how to capture particular moments, which made him the perfect choice for Tina Brown's first cover—that punk in the carriage. Even though the image conveyed Tina's attitude perfectly, it wasn't a specific assignment; the idea came from Sorel himself. He was able to adjust it to precisely what Brown was proposing for the magazine—a rejuvenation of the traditional approach. It's not as if the punk were running the carriage off the road; rather, he's a latter-day Tilley, lounging in the carriage and taking in the view (though the driver does look a bit disconcerted).

OCTOBER 5, 1992
by Edward Sorel

I ♥ BABEL by Edward Sorel
October 2, 1995

WALKERS AND GAWKERS by Edward Sorel
June 16, 1997

left:
KVETCH CITY
by Edward Sorel
January 31, 2000

below, left:
TIME AND TIDE
by Edward Sorel
April 10, 1995

When Sorel said that he was working on an image dealing with the impossibility of getting a cab at rush hour, the immediate reaction was: How can you do a cartoon of that? It was a good subject—New Yorkers would find it true—but how could it be represented? He did it through endless repetition. There are about a dozen clocks in the picture, and they all say a little after five o'clock, and the street is clogged with cabs, but they're all unavailable.

below, right:
EARLY BIRDS
by Edward Sorel
November 9, 1998

opposite:
CRUSH HOUR
by Edward Sorel
January 31, 1994

242ST-VAN CORTLA
OUTH FERRY
Edward Sorel

MASTERS OF THE UNIVERSE

left:

TUT'S TAXI
by Anita Kunz
March 10, 1997

below, left:

HANGING ON EVERY WORD
by J. J. Sempé
May 22, 2000

below, right:

A CERTAIN SENSE OF HIS OWN IMPORTANCE
by J. J. Sempé
February 2, 1998

opposite:

LENIN HAILS A CAB
by Vitaly Komar & Alexander Melamid
July 12, 1993

Komar and Melamid did this cover for a New Yorker issue that had an article about artists inventing new uses for suddenly obsolete Soviet monuments. But this cover could have run without the story—a cover should always have its own raison d'être, independent of whatever is inside. This image is a perfect juxtaposition of unexpected elements that, once seen, seem as though they were always meant to be together. Of course Lenin hails a cab in front of the Chrysler Building, which seems to be a Soviet monument, and of course the red flag has a McDonald's logo.

July 12, 1993

THE NEW YORKER

Price $1.95

Price $3.00

THE NEW YORKER

Jan. 10, 2000

opposite:
CENTER OF THE UNIVERSE by Mark Ulriksen
January 10, 2000

OCTOBER 11, 1930
by Theodore G. Haupt
The view from a biplane.

opposite:
CROSSTOWN TRAFFIC by Maira Kalman
December 4, 1995

THE TREASURE by Peter de Sève
July 17, 1995
Find the hidden treasures: Dorothy's ruby slippers, photos of aliens and Loch Ness monsters, Commandments XI-XIV, a dodo, a Rosebud sled . . .

125TH
57TH
42ND
14TH
CANA
Maira Kalman
0 321827 3 49
36340

Nov. 4, 1996

THE NEW YORKER

Price $2.95

MR

opposite:
THE HEIGHT OF FASHION by Michael Roberts
November 4, 1996

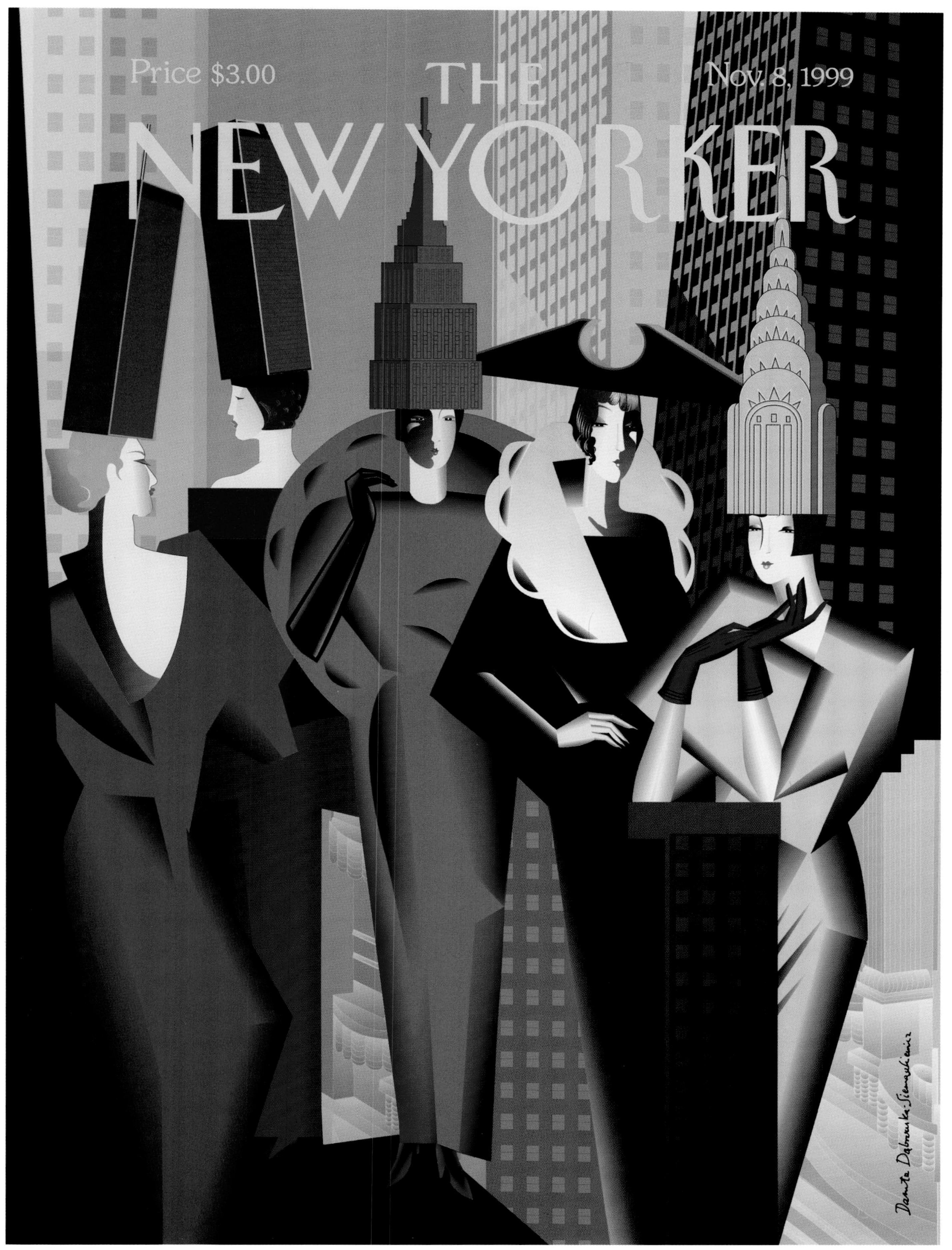

HIGH FASHION by Danuta Dabrowska-Siemaszkiewicz
November 8, 1999

LANDMARKS COMMISSION
TO MEET IN SPECIAL SESSION
by Bruce McCall, April 1, 1996

PHOTO OPPORTUNITY
by Bruce McCall
May 8, 2000

BRUCE McCALL

McCall is both an artist and a writer; he himself has trouble specifying which is his day job. Though he's now based in New York, he comes from Canada, and that slightly skewed foreigner's perspective (not to mention the peculiar tilt of his own point of view) leads him to question everything the rest of us New Yorkers pass by every day. "Blimp Park" was his first cover for us. I'd called him up in the early summer of 1993, after an accident involving a blimp in the streets of New York which had resulted in amazing tabloid photos of a building half wrapped in fluttering blimp skin. It seemed a perfect example of what we now think of as a McCall moment. He didn't disappoint, and he hasn't since. Those surreal pipes spewing steam in the middle of our congested streets? Only McCall seems to notice them, let alone penetrate their mystery.

BLIMP PARK by Bruce McCall
August 16, 1993

STEAMERS by Bruce McCall
November 21, 1994

King Kong Call by Bruce McCall
January 23, 1995

left:

BRONX CHEER
by Bruce McCall
October 18, 1993

At the time this image ran, there were discussions about moving Yankee Stadium out of the Bronx, but only McCall would have taken the idea literally.

below, left:

EASTER MORNING
by Bruce McCall
April 5, 1999

below, right:

THE SALE OF THE CENTURY
by Bruce McCall
February 3, 1997

opposite:

HAVE A NICE DAY
by Bruce McCall
March 7, 1994

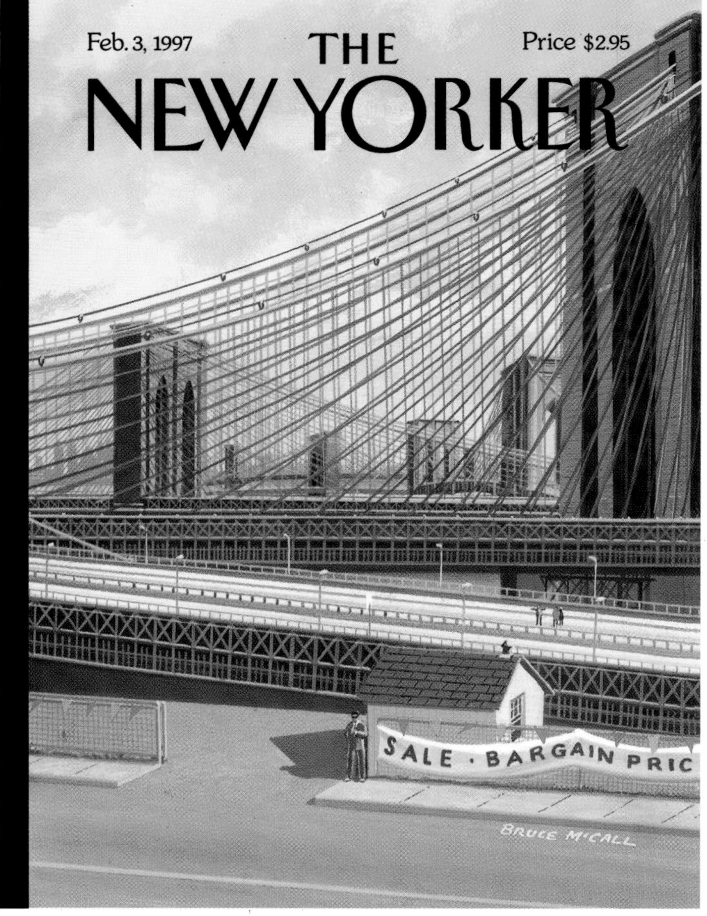

DRIVER LICEN
5 MIN. - NO
THE PORT AUTHO
BUS TERMI
"THE WORST S
"MISS IT AT ALL
S STONES
FREE
TONITE LIVE
WELCOME BACK, DODGERS!
CRUNCH ZONE
CARS WITH DIPLOMAT PLATES WILL BE COMPACTED
YOUR WA
ZOO
90
anadian
CUISINE
HERE TO?
TAXI
POLLYANNA
NICE CLOTHIN
$100 FINE
IF YOU DON'T HAVE A NICE DAY
TAXI
STANDING - ANY TIME ANY PLACE
PEACE
LOVE
BRUCE McCALL

JULY 15, 1944
by Rea Irvin

CATCHING THE MOMENT

BLACK IN AMERICA
by Michael Roberts
April 29 & May 6, 1996

opposite:
SOCIAL LIGHTS by M. Scott Miller
September 23, 1996

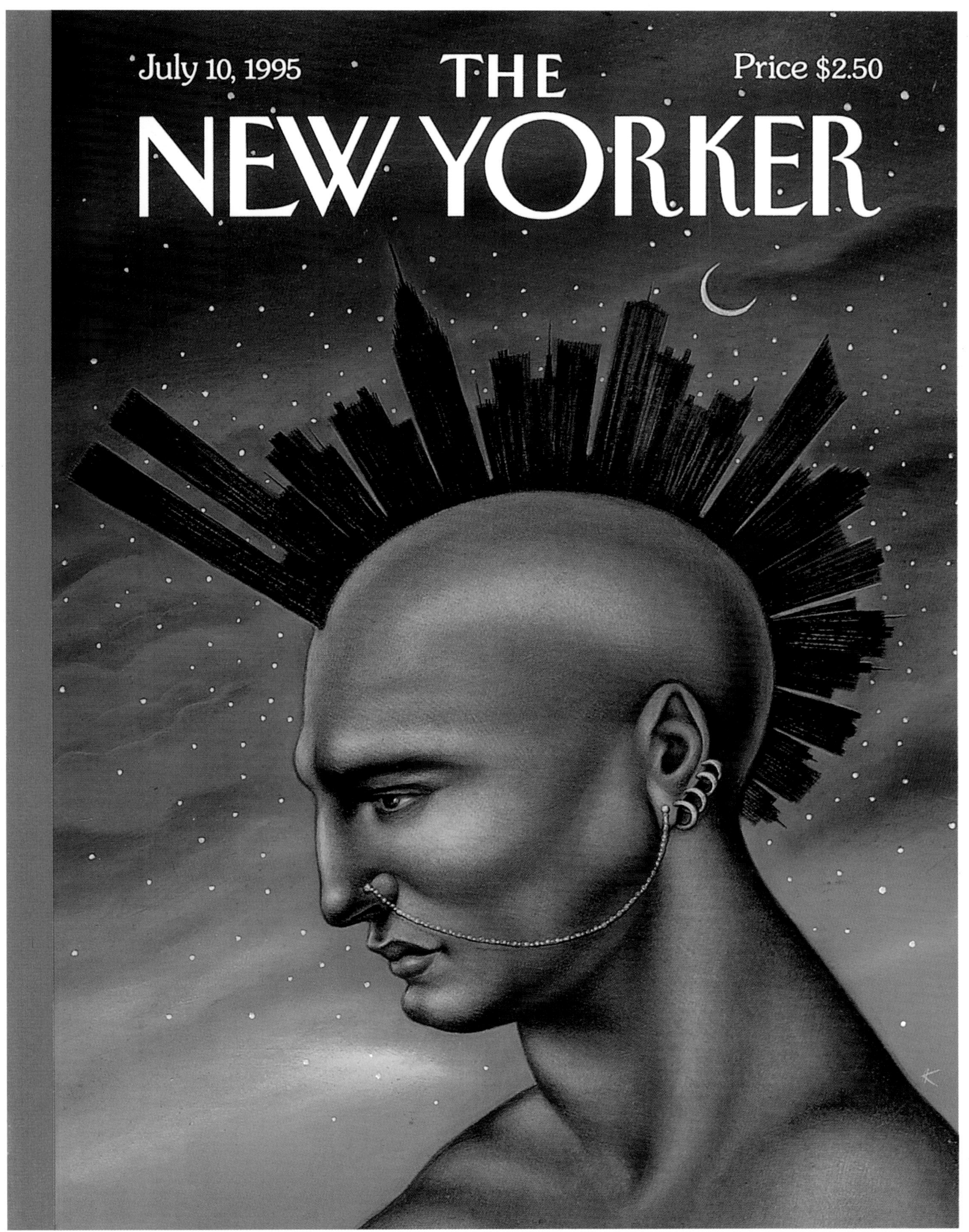

MOHAWK MANHATTAN by Anita Kunz
July 10, 1995

opposite:
WORK STATION, PLAY STATION by J. Otto Seibold
December 6, 1999

BIG BABY by Carter Goodrich
October 18 & 25, 1999
When this cover ran, everyone was worrying about Y2K.

DEATH
SEX
PORNO
CLICK NOW
SEX
SEX
SEX
PLAY AGAIN?
GAME OVER
SLUTS
SEX
SEX
SEX
DEATH
SEX
KILL
MONDAY SUCKS

UPDATING THE TRADITION

left:

BACK IN THE NEW WORLD
by Jacques de Loustal
October 11, 1993

It's sometimes hard to turn an idea into a successful image. This cover referred to an incident in which several people had drowned when a boat carrying illegal Chinese immigrants capsized off Queens. Putting this worn and patched vessel in the middle of a sailboat race got the incongruity but failed to capture the tragedy. It's so harmoniously painted that a lot of people saw it as just another beautiful, traditional cover.

below, left:

HACKING IT
by R. Sikoryak
September 25, 1995

below, right:

EINSTEIN, ZWEISTEIN, DREISTEIN
by Maira Kalman
April 7, 1997

opposite:

When R. Crumb sent this in, we noticed that it showed the view in front of our old offices on Forty-second Street, but we didn't realize that it was also a play on Rea Irvin's Eustace Tilley. Crumb had sent it to us without comment. This was the image that broke with the sixty-eight-year tradition of putting Irvin's Tilley on every anniversary issue.
We got hundreds of irate letters, which absolutely delighted Crumb.

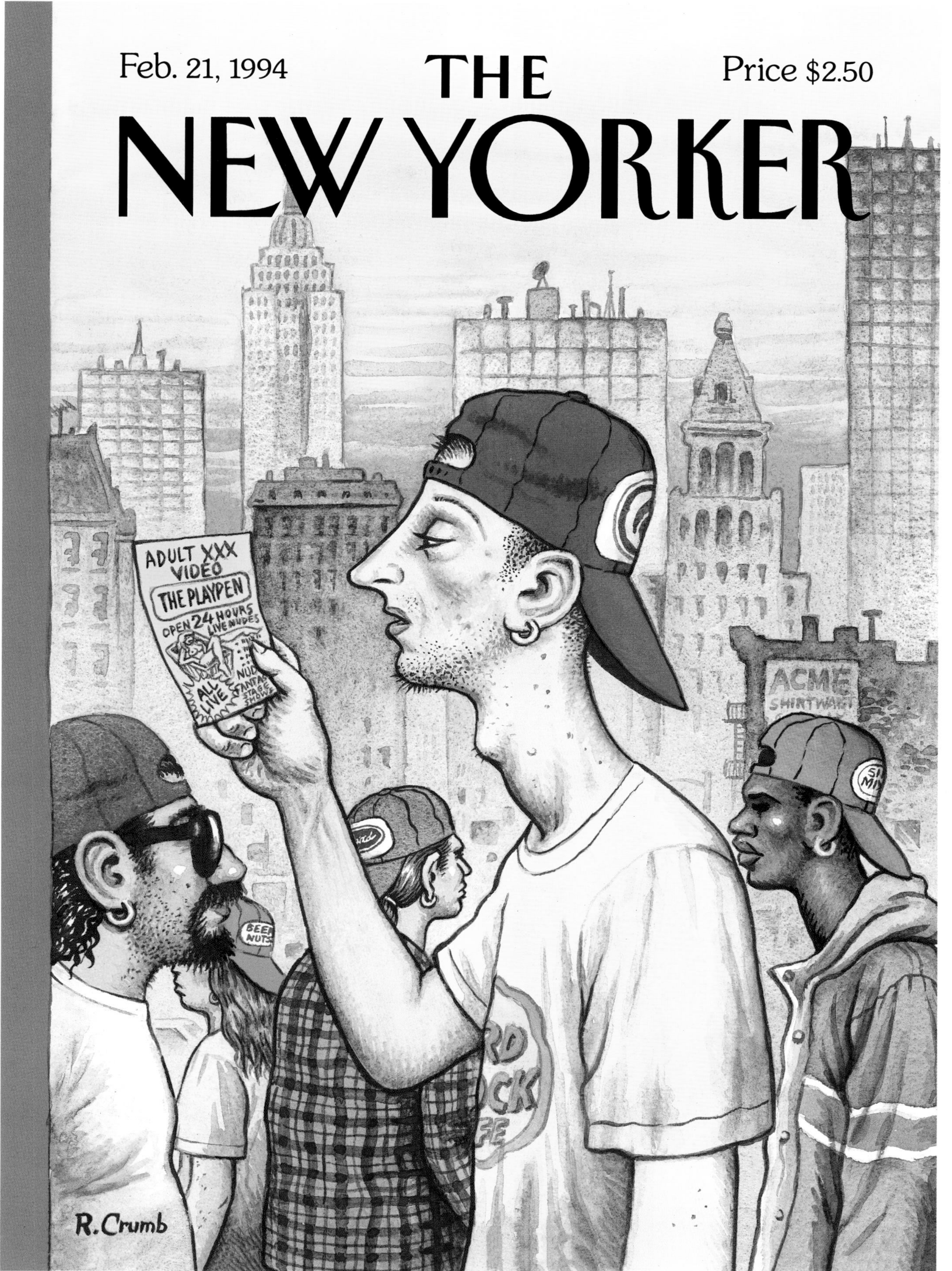

ELVIS TILLEY by R. Crumb
February 21, 1994

CURRENT EVENTS

left:

CASTLES IN THE SAND
by David Mazzucchelli
July 26, 1993

Commenting on the World Trade Center bombing, Mazzucchelli portrayed a freckle-faced kid destroying a sand castle with twin towers. Although the artist included a boy with Semitic features who is as appalled as the others at this act of terrorism, the magazine nevertheless received bomb threats.

left:

DISTRACTED
by Barry Blitt
July 25, 1994

While the O. J. case had made it into the magazine, it seemed daunting to deal with such a sensational topic on the cover. Then Barry Blitt sent in a sketch of this image. At the time, everybody was watching TV; more interesting than whether O.J. was guilty or not guilty was the fact that it seemed to be a shared moment of mass hysteria.

This was an image that would have been funny, that could have been a New Yorker cover, even if O. J.'s face had been erased from the picture. And that made it perfect for a New Yorker cover on the topic.

opposite:

The only other O. J. cover we ran was an equally classic New Yorker cover.

A BIT OF O.J. TO START THE DAY by HA (Bob Zoell)
January 30, 1995

opposite:
LAST SALUTE by R. Sikoryak
September 15, 1997

ON THE BEACH by R. Sikoryak
January 26, 1998
This ran during Pope John Paul II's visit to Cuba.
opposite: Mourning the death of Princess Diana.

R. SIKORYAK

ON TRACK
by Barry Blitt
September 19, 1994

THE COMMUTER
by Barry Blitt
March 16, 1998

BARRY BLITT

Blitt has a career as a cartoonist and an illustrator, and he's also done comic strips for various magazines and newspapers. He's good at capturing the feelings we all have about how hard it is to keep up with the pace of modern life. His style is casual and loose, but he works very hard—for a single picture he'll make five or six finished versions, doing the same sketch different ways, all with slight variations. Since he doesn't like to patch his drawings, if there's a single part that he doesn't like he redoes the entire picture. Yet he manages to retain the looseness of the initial sketch in the final version, and the sense of spontaneity that he has been able to preserve adds to the humor; it gives you the feeling that the artist had such a great idea he couldn't wait to show it to you.

DON'T ASK by Barry Blitt
June 17, 1996

THE POPE IN THE CITY by Barry Blitt
October 9, 1995

BUZZ CITY by Barry Blitt
September 27, 1999
This was the moment when the West Nile virus invaded New York.

left:
UPWARDLY MOBILE
by Barry Blitt
May 16, 1994

below, left:
RIDES OF MARCH
by Barry Blitt
March 13, 1995

below, right:
LOCKED UP
by Barry Blitt
November 17, 1997

opposite:
When businesses began to severely limit smoking in offices, various artists proposed images dealing with what was then the new sight of people huddled in front of buildings smoking. A typical suggestion used a huge cloud of smoke to make the point. Barry's proposal added another dimension. The drawing emphasizes not just the fact that people have to go outside to smoke but also the suicidal impulse of those who smoke and the isolation that has been imposed on them—what was once a social activity now makes people pariahs.

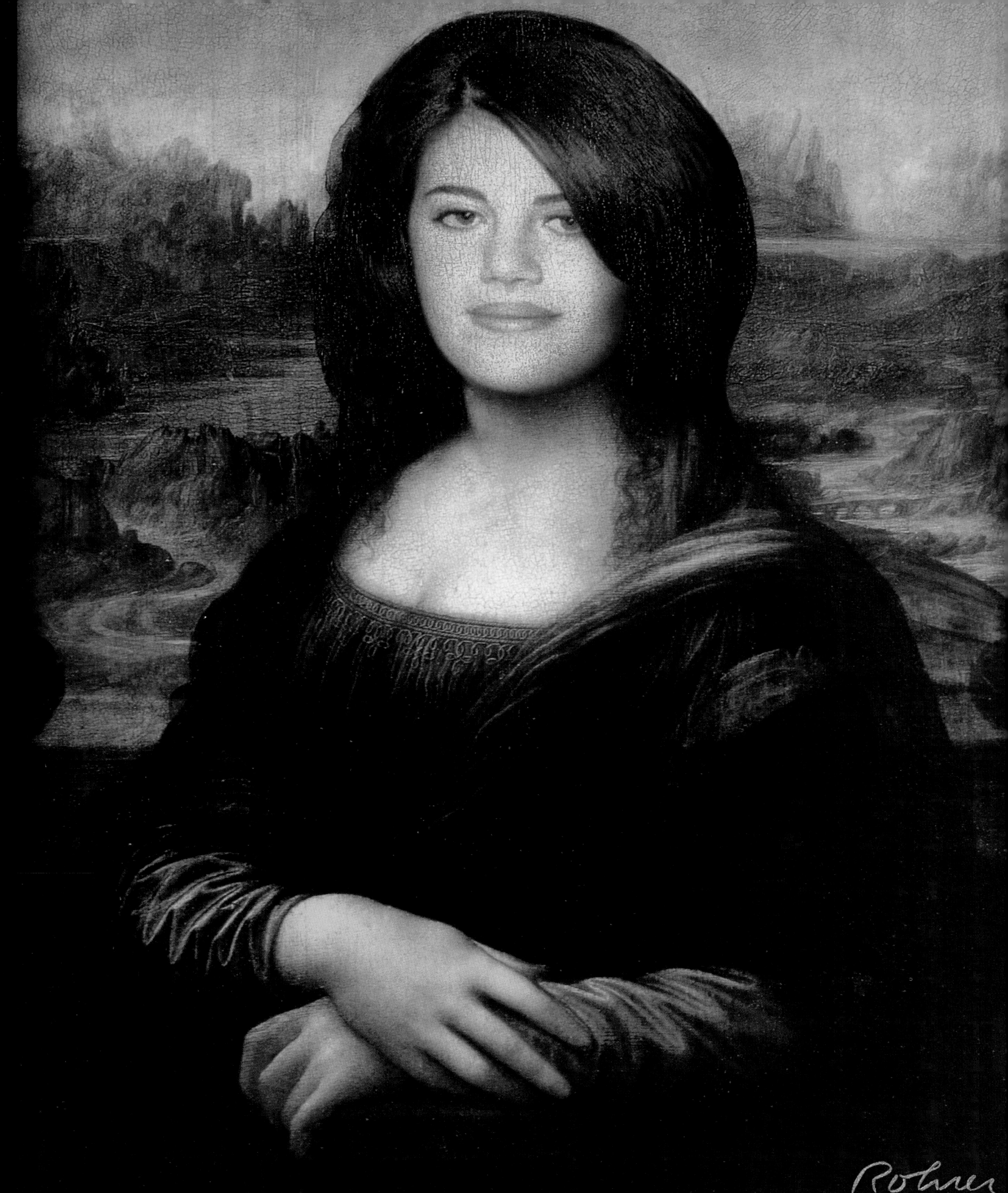
Rohner

left:

ALL THE NEWS UNFIT TO PRINT
by Edward Sorel
September 28, 1998

far left:

THE ARENA
by Edward Sorel
November 14, 1994

below, left:

THE TOUGH GUY AND THE TOURIST
by Harry Bliss
July 19, 1999

This image captured an early moment in the prospective race for the U.S. Senate between Mayor Rudolph Giuliani and Hillary Clinton. It was so evenhanded that it couldn't have been co-opted by either candidate.

below, right:

JULY 10, 1948
by Peter Arno

THE LOW ROAD by Art Spiegelman
February 16, 1998
This appeared around the time the Lewinsky affair was first breaking.

COVER STORIES & SPECIAL ISSUES

The New Yorker began occasionally running covers linked to a story inside in 1993 and special issues devoted to a particular topic—from fiction to fashion to money—in 1994.

right:
AMERICA, AMERICA
by Winston Smith
August 23 & 30, 1999
for the Adventure issue

far right:
WHERE THE HEART IS
by Ana Juan
October 16, 1995
for the Home issue

right:
UNDER THE CLOUD
by Lorenzo Mattotti
July 31, 1995
fifty years after Hiroshima

below:
STRANGERS IN THE NIGHT
by Edward Sorel
November 3, 1997
for "Sinatra Song,"
a profile by John Lahr

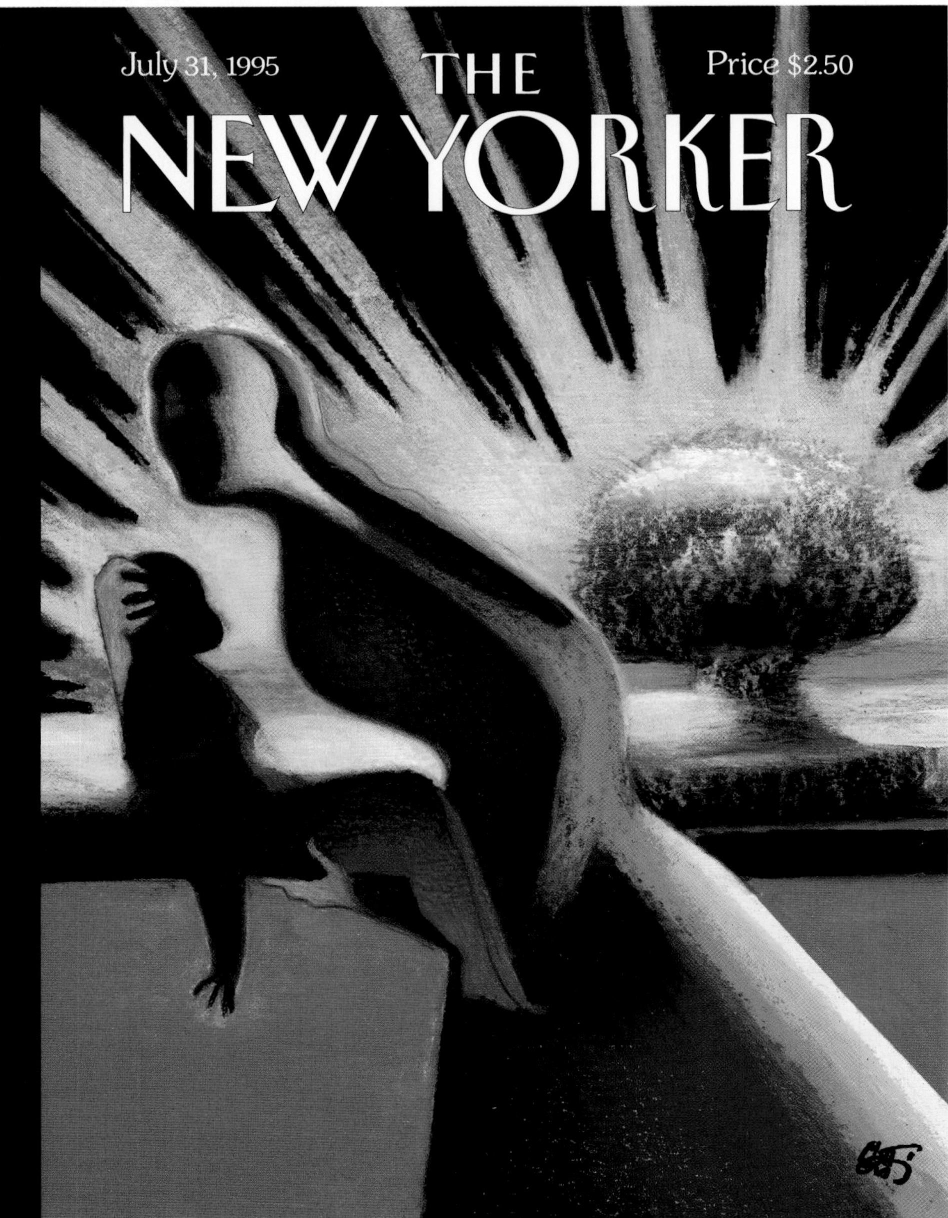

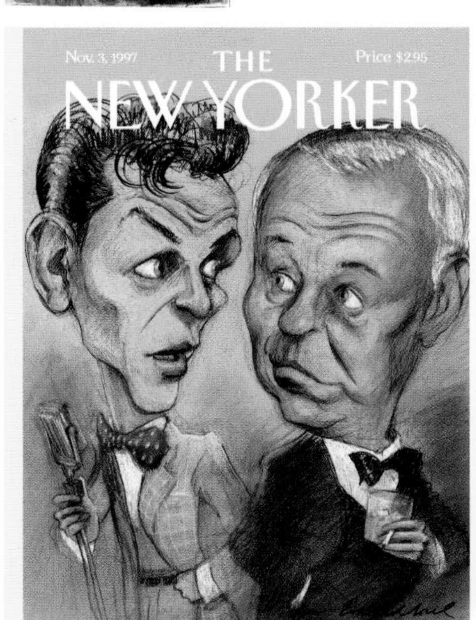

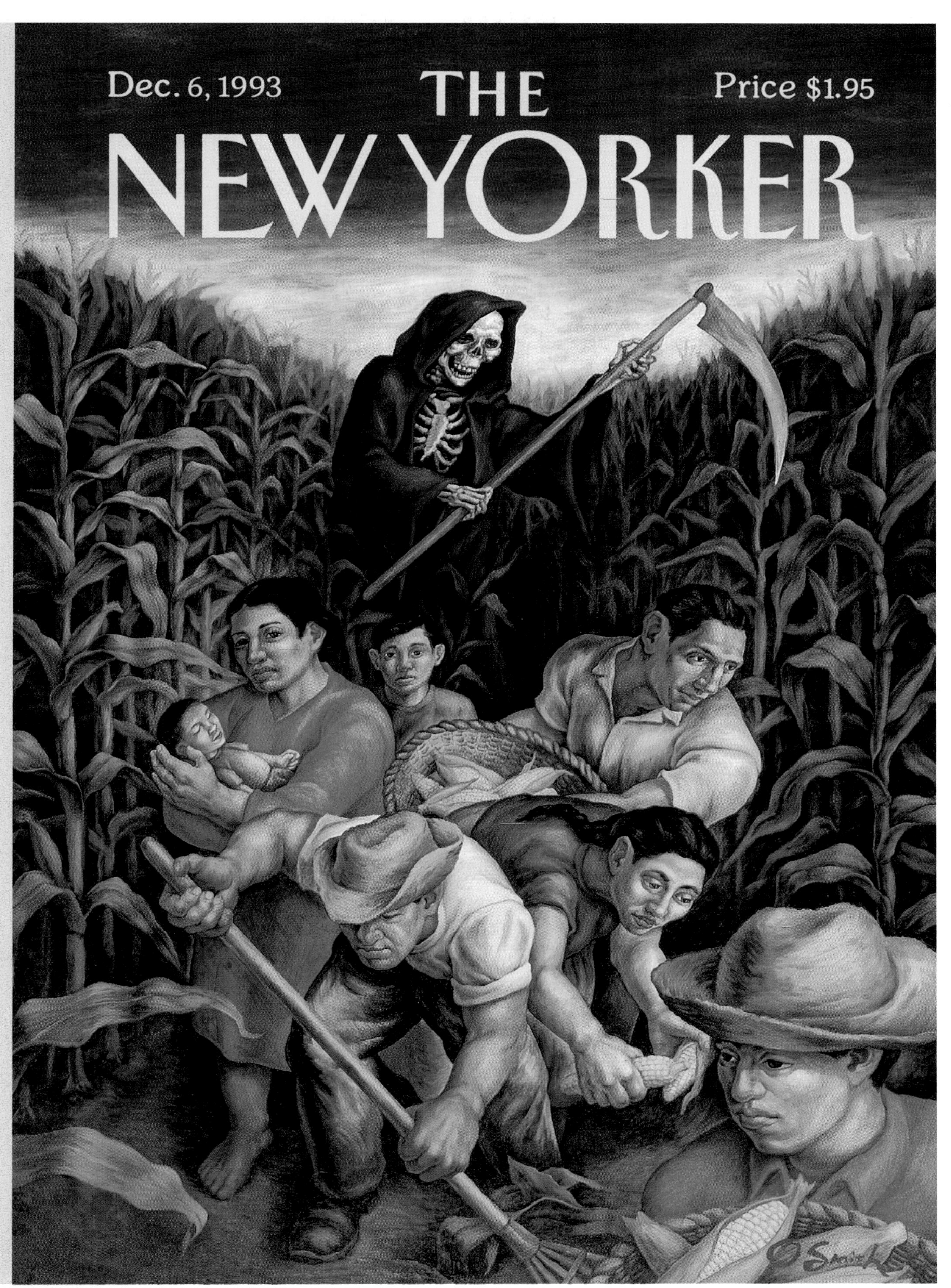

IN THE FIELD by Owen Smith
December 6, 1993
This issue featured Mark Danner's report on a massacre in El Mozote, El Salvador.

opposite:
THE MONEY TREE by Winston Smith
April 24 & May 1, 2000

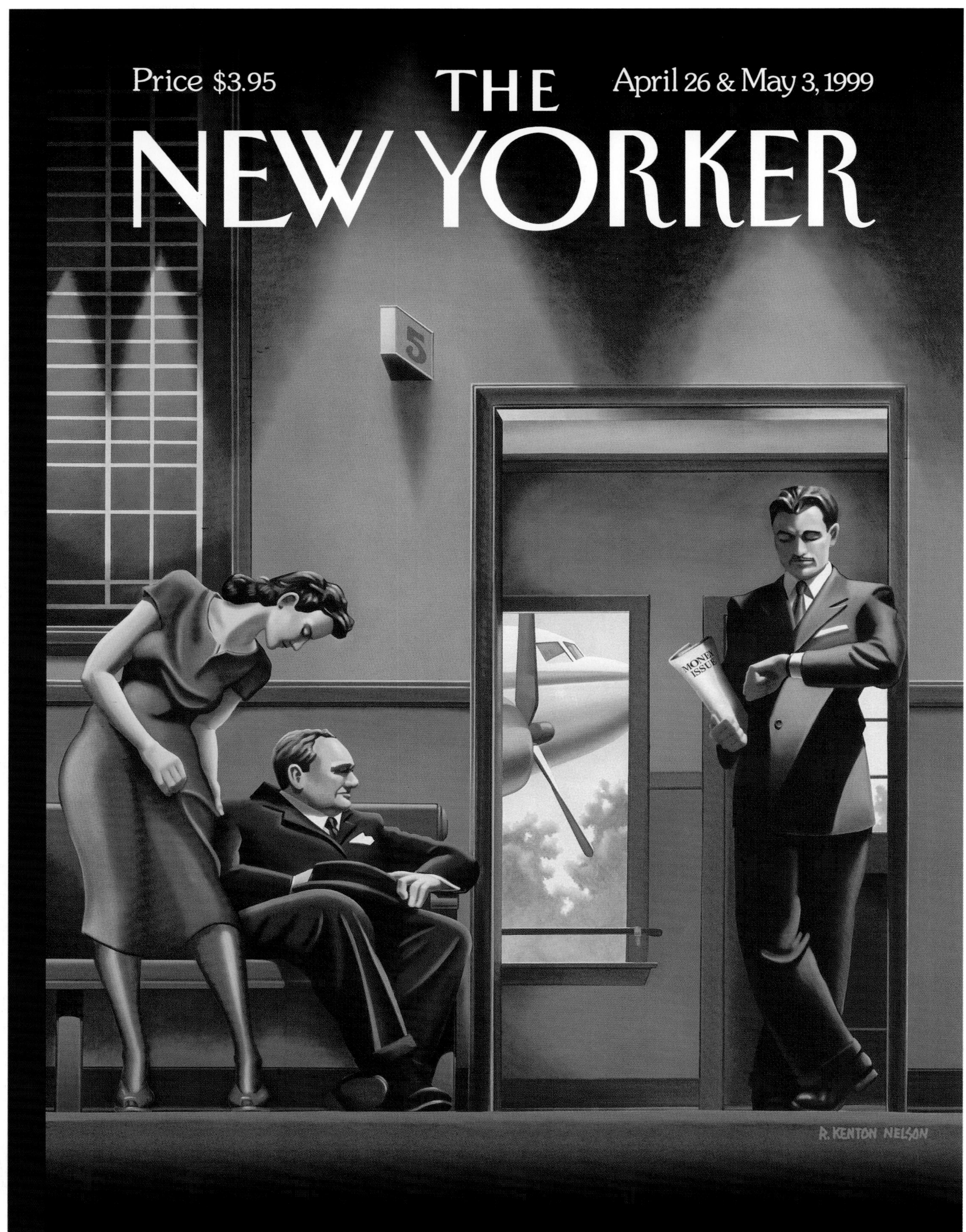

TIME IS MONEY by R. Kenton Nelson
April 26 & May 3, 1999
Two different covers for special issues on money.
opposite: The moment of irrational exuberance.

STON
MITH

THEOLOGY OF THE TAX CUT
by Art Spiegelman
April 17, 1995

"M" IS FOR THE MANY THINGS SHE GAVE ME
by Art Spiegelman, May 10, 1993

ART SPIEGELMAN

One of the first artists Tina Brown brought in was Art Spiegelman, whose Holocaust survivor's tale, "Maus," had recently won a Pulitzer Prize. He had come out of underground comix and had been in the vanguard of publishing strong storytelling images, in cartoons as well as comic strips. Spiegelman quickly became a lightning rod for critics of the new *New Yorker.* Some of his covers were enormously controversial (and were the occasion for many cancelled subscriptions), although often the real scandal was in the subject he was addressing rather than in his treatment of it. A master at compressing explosive images, he sometimes condenses them to the point that, when they do go off, debris scatters in all directions. But the idea is never just to destroy something; if anything, it is to provoke a long-overdue dialogue.

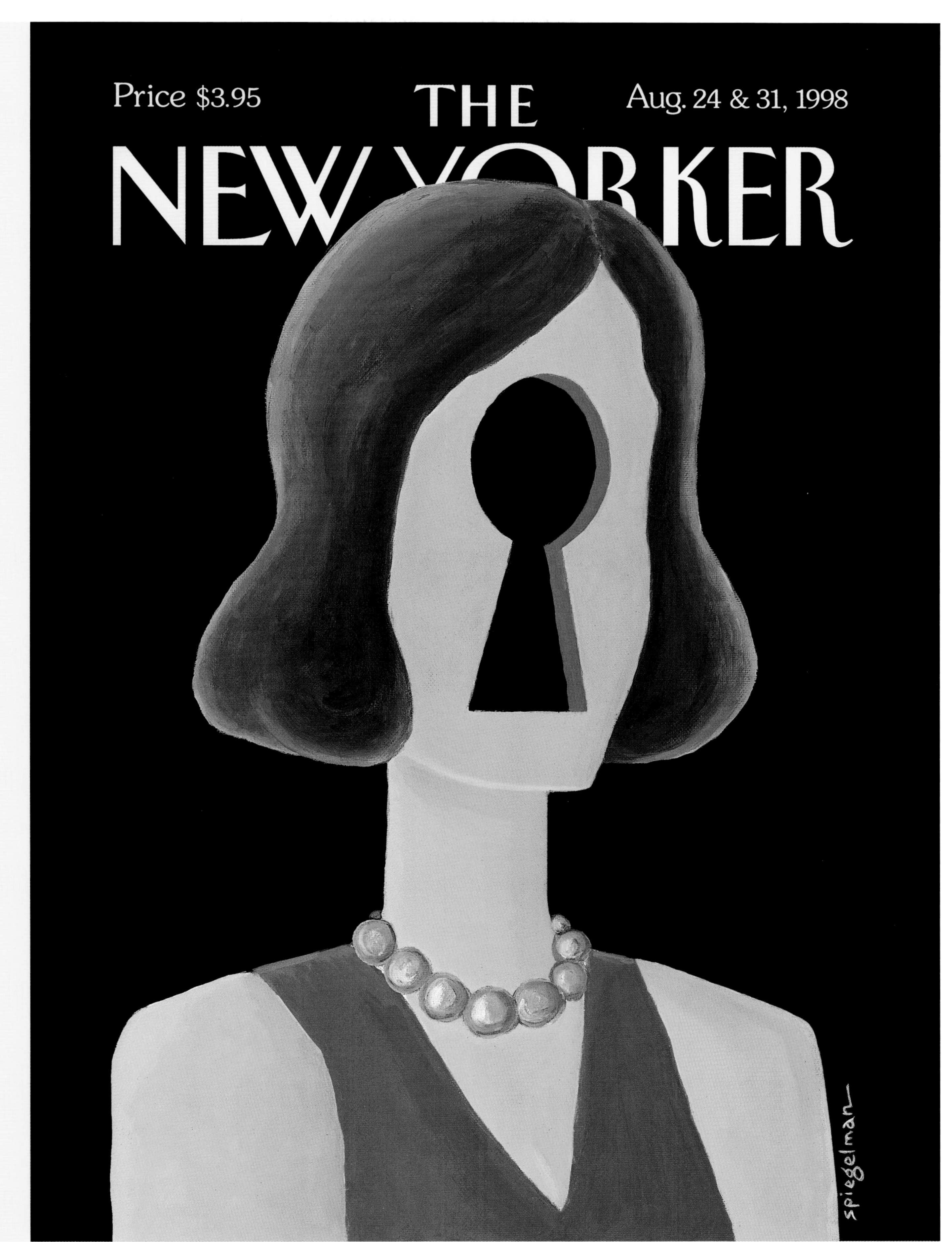

PRIVATE LIVES by Art Spiegelman
August 24 & 31, 1998

BEAU AND EROS by Art Spiegelman
August 25 & September 1, 1997

DICK TILLEY by Art Spiegelman
February 24 & March 3, 1997

left:
BRIEF ENCOUNTER
by Art Spiegelman
September 26, 1994

below, left:
PROCESSED PEACE
by Art Spiegelman
October 14, 1996

below, right:
FARSIGHTED
by Art Spiegelman
October 20 & 27, 1997

41 *SHOTS* 10¢ by Art Spiegelman
March 8, 1999
Amadou Diallo, an African immigrant, had been killed by New York City police officers. He had been shot at forty-one times.

HAPPY NEW YEAR
WELCOME 1998

A YEAR AT THE NEW YORKER

DECEMBER 30, 1933
by Rea Irvin

opposite:
THE NEW YEAR by Harry Bliss
January 5, 1998

NEW YEAR

clockwise from right:
HAPPY NEW YEAR
by Richard McGuire
December 27, 1993 &
January 3, 1994
(two views)

CHANGING FORTUNES
by Edward Sorel
January 8, 1996

opposite, clockwise from top left:
JANUARY 1, 1944
by Peter Arno

HAPPY NEW YEAR
by HA (Bob Zoell)
December 26, 1994 &
January 2, 1995

DECEMBER 31, 1949
by Mary Petty

JANUARY 2, 1932
by Rea Irvin
It was Irvin who drew the extraordinarily resilient New Yorker logo, and here he gave himself the freedom to play with it.

Jan. 1, 1944
THE NEW YORKER
Price 15 cents
Peter Arno

Dec. 26, 1994
Jan. 2, 1995
THE NEW YORKER
Price $2.95

Jan. 2, 1932
THE NEW YORKER
Price 15 cents
REA IRVIN

Dec. 31, 1949
THE NEW YORKER
Price 20 cents

opposite:
SPYGLASS by Lorenzo Mattotti
January 11, 1999

NIGHTHAWKS NEW YEAR by Owen Smith
December 27, 1999 & January 3, 2000
The millennial cover.

Saul Steinberg would work and rework his images until he got them to the point where they "settled" for him. The first sketch (left) for his "2000" cover was done in 1994, with the ensuing years spaced out on the road to the new millennium. By the time the cover ran, in January, 1997 (opposite), Steinberg had been playing with the idea for two years, and his sketches show how his mood shifted. Another 1994 sketch (below, left) has a less tempestuous, more hopeful sky. The artist also reconsidered the road itself: a 1996 sketch (below, right) shows a more tortuous route; the simplified version that ran preserved a loop where the road encircles itself, and past and future join. Steinberg died in the spring of 1999.

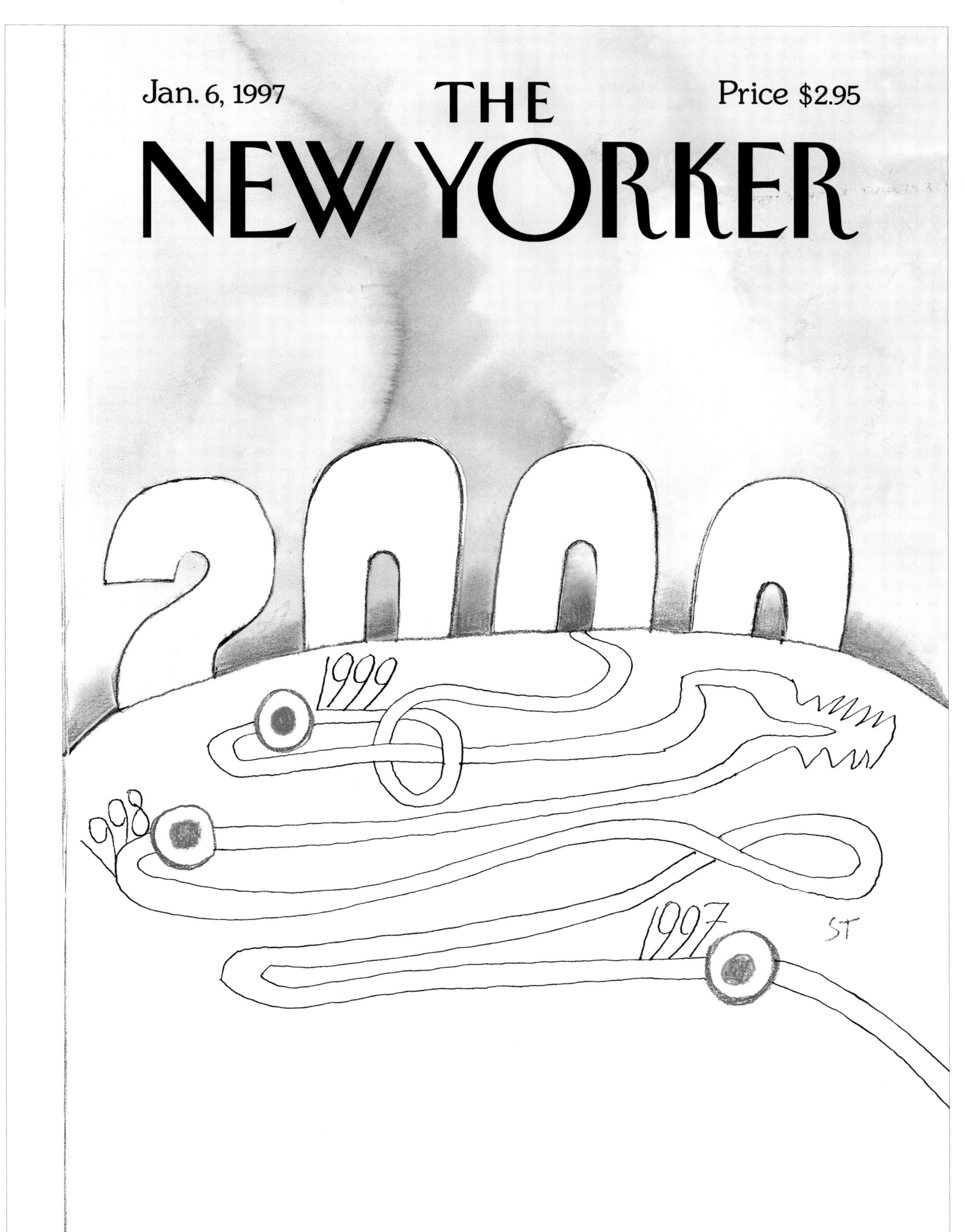

2000 by Saul Steinberg
January 6, 1997

WINTER

clockwise from right:
CITY SKATE
by Lorenzo Mattotti
January 13, 1997

SNOW HAUL
by Lorenzo Mattotti
January 9, 1995

THE DIEHARD CAFÉ
by Kathy Osborn
January 17, 1994

opposite, clockwise from top left:
SNOW SMOKING
by Art Spiegelman
January 15, 1996

ICE BURG
by David Sandlin
January 22, 1996

WINTER IS SPRUNG
by Raúl Colón
March 27, 2000

HOT, HOT, HOT
by Art Spiegelman
January 27, 1997

Jan. 15, 1996
THE NEW YORKER
Price $2.95
art spiegelman

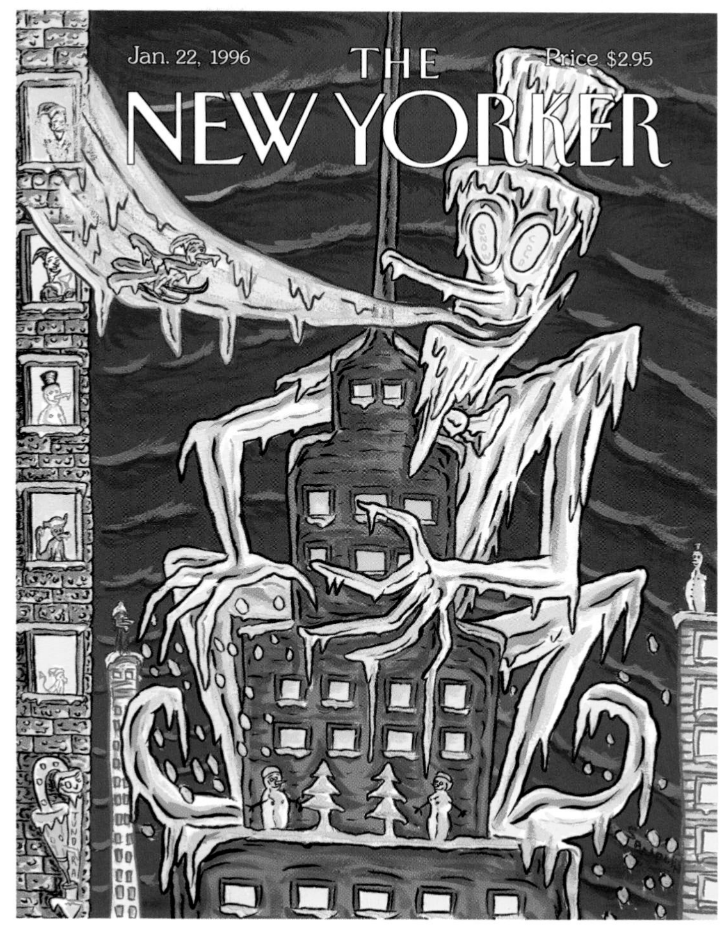
Jan. 22, 1996
THE NEW YORKER
Price $2.95

Jan. 27, 1997
THE NEW YORKER
Price $2.95
XXX
VIDEO
HOT!
HOT
HOT!

PRICE $3.00
THE NEW YORKER
MAR. 27, 2000

opposite:
WARM FRONT by Lorenzo Mattotti
March 11, 1996

TAILED by Peter de Sève
January 24, 1994

left:
MARCH 1, 1941
by Constantin Alajálov

below, left:
OLÉ
by Floc'h
February 10, 1997

below, right:
UNDER BRIDGES
by Eric Drooker
March 6, 1995

opposite:
THROUGH THE PARK, JAMES
by Peter de Sève
January 19, 1998

left:

UP THE DOWN SLOPE
by Harry Bliss
January 24, 2000

It was the work of Charles Addams, among others, that made Harry Bliss want to become a cartoonist. He had already handed in the image at left when two skiing accidents involving celebrities and trees occurred. Someone suggested replacing the upward-bound skier with a tree (above, left). Bliss tried that, but preferred having the tree chasing the skier (above, center); a third sketch (above, right) responded even more directly to the recent events. Good taste prevailed; we ended up running the original image, but not until much later.

below:

DOWN THE HILL
by Ian Falconer
January 25, 1999

FEBRUARY 2, 1957
by Charles Addams

MARTIN LUTHER KING DAY

right:
THE LIFE OF MARTIN LUTHER KING, JR.
by Edward Sorel
January 18, 1999

opposite:
I HAD A DREAM
by Mark Ulriksen
January 16, 1995

left:
HAILING DR. KING
by Barry Blitt
January 17, 2000

Barry Blitt proposed this image when the actor Danny Glover was making news with his complaints about the number of empty cabs that passed him by—an experience familiar to many black men in New York City.

FREE AT LAST
ulriksen

VALENTINE'S DAY

left:

FEBRUARY 15, 1936
by William Steig

Times change: although this image of a young boy mooning over a grown woman was no doubt seen as innocent in its day, it might elicit a different reaction if it were to be published now.

below, left:

FEBRUARY 13, 1960
by Leonard Dove

below, right:

FEBRUARY 9, 1929
by Helen E. Hokinson

VALENTINE'S DAY by Art Spiegelman
February 15, 1993
This cover ran at a time when tensions were high between the Hasidim and Caribbean blacks in the Crown Heights section of Brooklyn.

CUPID'S VOLLEY by Peter de Sève
February 19, 1996

FEBRUARY 12, 1944; FEBRUARY 10, 1951; FEBRUARY 11, 1961; FEBRUARY 16, 1981
by Charles Addams

left:

VALENTINES
by Mark Ulriksen
February 14, 2000

Art Spiegelman's controversial 1993 Valentine's Day cover becomes a decorative motif in 2000 in a process reminiscent of the Kafka parable: leopards break into the temple and drink to the dregs what is in the sacrificial pitchers; eventually, the leopards become part of the ceremony.

far left:

FUNNY VALENTINE
by Mariscal
February 14, 1994

left:

GHOULS RUSH IN
by Edward Sorel
February 17, 1997

opposite:

HEART ATTACK
by Ian Falconer
February 15, 1999

One of our editors was on the phone with his bank, speaking with a clerk in the Midwest, and when he told her that he worked at The New Yorker she replied, "Oh, The New Yorker! I love that magazine. What I really loved was that cover you had last Valentine's Day with Cupid as a little sniper. I liked it so much I had the image tattooed on my breast."

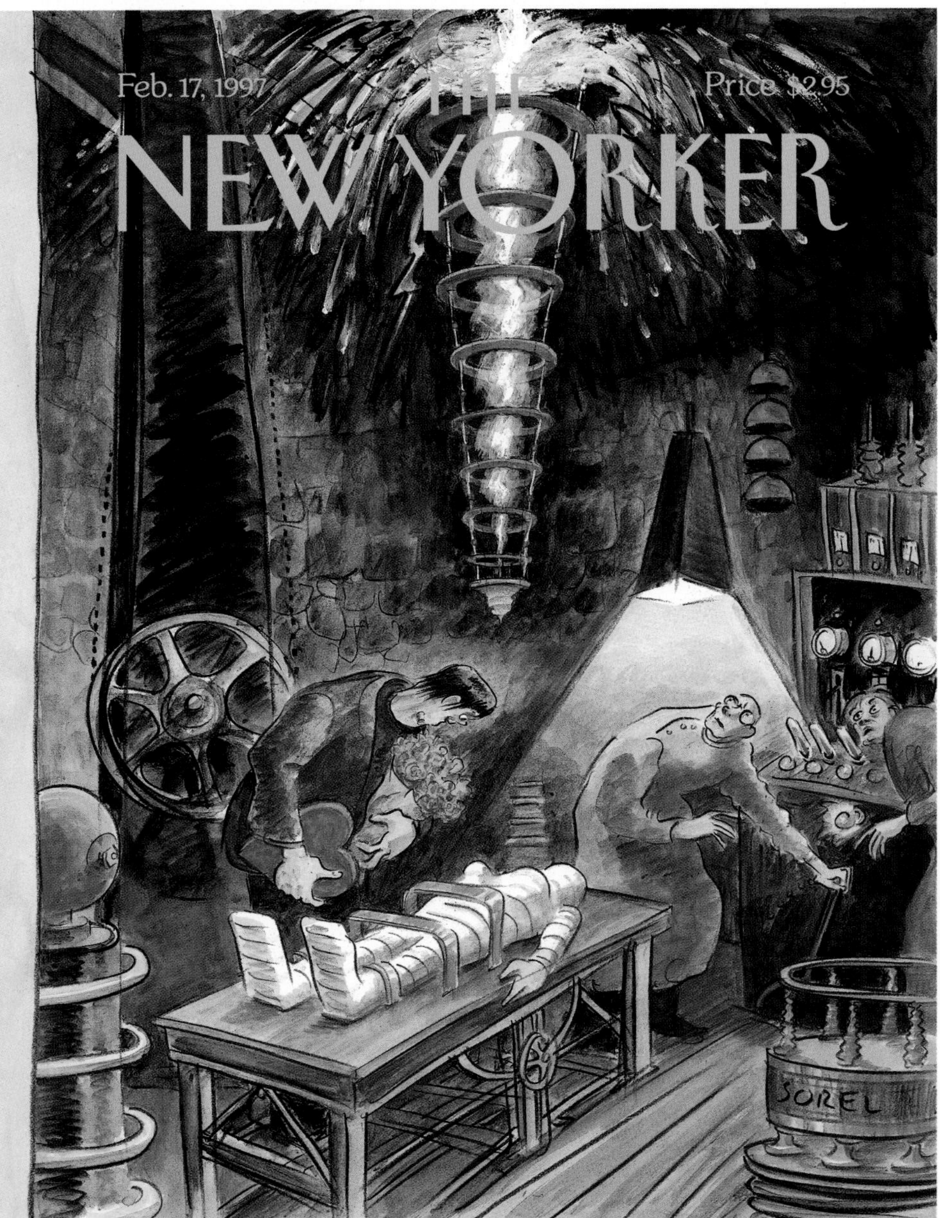

Falconer

ST. PATRICK'S DAY

clockwise from right:

ST. PATRICK'S DAY: BROOMSTICK OF THE LORD
by Sue Coe
March 15, 1993
In 1993, gay activists rallied against the ban on gay groups' marching in the St. Patrick's Day parade.

MARCH 19, 1938
by Will Cotton
One of the remarkably few examples of racial and ethnic stereotyping in the old New Yorker, though such imagery was prevalent in the advertisements and cartoons of the day.

MARCH 18, 1933
by William Steig

MARCH 16, 1935
by Constantin Alajálov

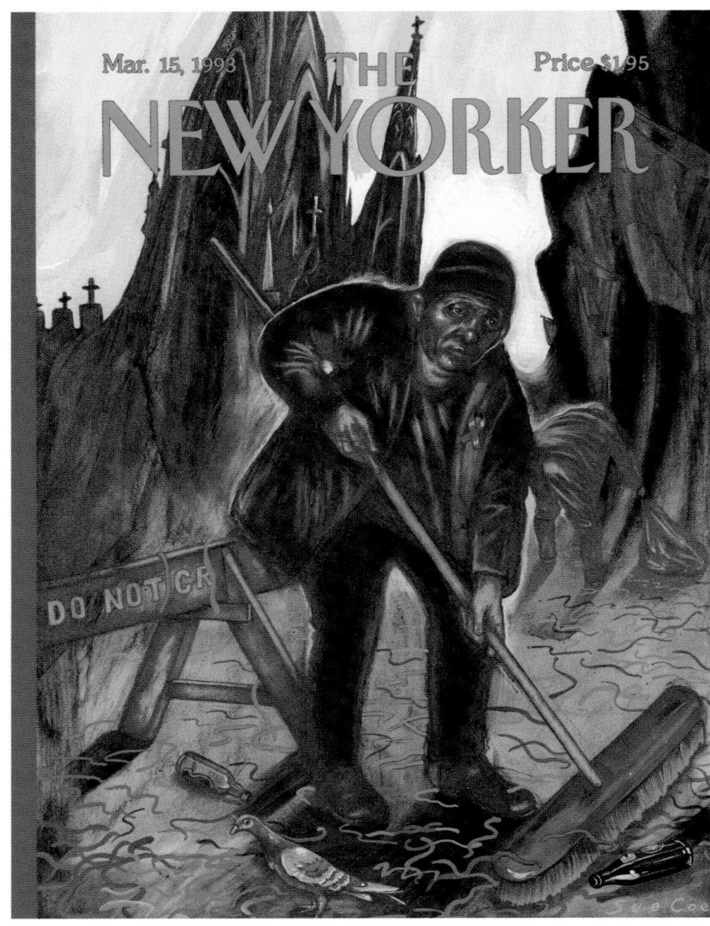

APRIL FOOLS' DAY

NINETY-FIVE FOOLS

by Richard McGuire
April 3, 1995

Richard McGuire created a cover containing at least ninety-five pranks. Some readers counted as many as ninety-nine.

April is misspelled, the date is corrected by hand, and the year has an extra "9." In the top left corner, a water tower takes off as a rocket, a crane has been converted into a ticktacktoe board, and a small airplane trails a sign reading "April Fool" backward.

The first "r" in "New Yorker" is reversed. A man clings to the edge of the moon, and to his left a man sits on a beam suspended from the crane's cable. The dot over the "i" in "Price" has become an eye.

In the top right-hand corner, a man walks out of an open window. Below him, a man hangs upside down. Lower still, a man steps out one window and into another, and a window frame becomes a hanging picture frame. A cat hangs from a window through which little waves can be seen. A crocodile waits with open jaws, and a saw slices through the side of the building.

Under the date, a billboard model with only one arm and leg extends the leg onto a nearby traffic signal, which has too many lights. A precariously balanced bucket of water topples over. On the light pole street signs point to "Nowhere" and "Anywhere"; a "One Way" sign points in two directions; and a small bird bisects the pole.

The crosswalk sign reads "April Fool" backward. A man walks head first into the pole as a two-headed bird looks on.

On the left, a woman carries a chair in which a monkey sits, holding a jack-in-the-box. The woman, donning dark glasses, appears twice more: at the far left, where her midsection is missing, and at the bottom of the page, where she is riding in a bus driven by a baby. The other passengers on the bus are a woman with eyes in her hairdo and a man with a round head who is reading an upside-down book. The horn on the bus is doubled by a quacking duck, and a tiny woman in a wheelchair holds on to the rear of the bus for dear life.

In front of the bus are a small man holding a beam and a lizard riding a bicycle near a sewer grate, from which two eyes peek. Above, an old woman wearing a flower-pot hat, a bra, and three-eyed glasses walks an upside-down dog. A two-fingered man sporting headphones but no Walkman walks with legs parallel to the ground. In front of him is a man with a tail. There is a mysterious lump in the pavement behind him. Above, a tiny man is lifting the corner of a building off its foundation.

In the building, a skeleton works at a newsstand, which displays a picture of a man smoking six cigars. A boy hangs upside down next to one of the magazines. At the entrance to the building, a revolving door splits a man in two. Above the door is an elevator dial.

A woman being chased by a cell phone is about to slip on a banana peel. A periscope eye sticks up from a flooded subway entrance. The globe that marks the subway entrance has been replaced by a fishbowl. Above, a black mouse flies a blimp. The blimp trails a tightrope, and a miniature woman holding an umbrella walks out a window onto it. Nearby, a bird smokes a cigarette, and another pecks a hole in the side of the building.

Below, a faceless woman and her daughter, who carries her head as a balloon, walk down the street. A man leans out a crooked window. The back half of a deer crosses behind a deer-crossing sign. A three-legged police officer watches.

In front of him are a fire hydrant with feet and a miniature car speeding down the street. A faucet on the side of the building spouts water upward. An anthropomorphized clock crawls on the sidewalk. A glass and a bottle hold hands as they walk along. On the curb is a trash can containing a leg.

A two-wheeled taxi has two drivers. One door says "Taxi," the other "Toxi." One of the wheels is square, and the other has a square hubcap. A face peers out from under the taxi. Below, a mouse—similar to the one flying the blimp—rides a stick of dynamite. The mouse's tail is lighted instead of the fuse.

Below the title, a wedding cake looms next to a leaning tower of Pisa, and a man fishes off the side of a building. A man rows a boat above a window, suspended in midair. Below is a cactus falling upward.

In the center of the picture, the Devil sticks his head up out of a manhole, a miniature man runs across the street, shielding his head with a coin, and a one-armed man tips both his hat and his head. A man crossing the street has a disconnected left foot. Two eyes peek out of his pocket. The cover of the magazine he's holding shows him after the bucket above him has fallen on his head.

SPRING

left:
APRIL 25, 1959
by Abe Birnbaum

below, left:
MARCH 2, 1935
by Robert J. Day

below, right:
STOP AND SMELL THE FLOWERS
by Peter de Sève
April 11, 1994

Although Peter de Sève is in his early forties, his drawings sometimes evoke the wistfulness of an older man.

opposite:
À LA RECHERCHE DU PRINTEMPS PERDU
by William Steig
May 24, 1993

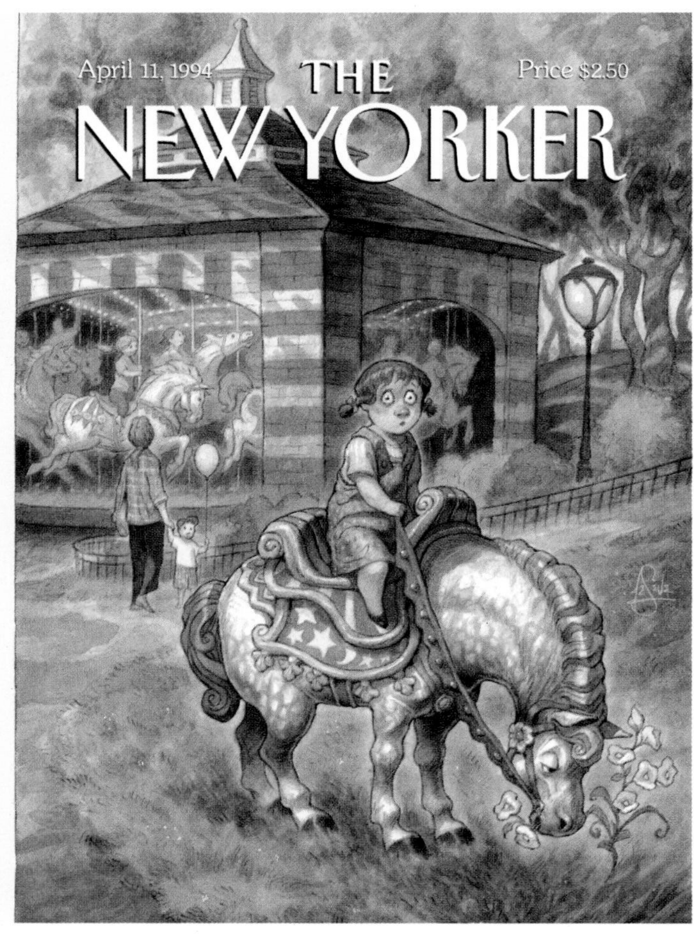

W. Steig

right:
A Spin in the Country
by Ever Meulen
May 23, 1994

below, left:
Out Like a Lamb
by Art Spiegelman
March 6, 2000

below, right:
The Great Outdoors
by Benoît van Innis
May 27, 1996

opposite:
Reap What You Sow
by William Joyce
May 17, 1999
William Joyce's characters all have distinct personalities, like those in the forties drawings that inspire this highly respected children's-book artist.

EASTER

right:
MARCH 28, 1959
by Charles Addams

below, left:
HARDBOILED EGG HUNT
by Art Spiegelman
March 31, 1997

below, right:
THE EGG MAN
by William Joyce
April 4, 1994

opposite:
ANOTHER DAY,
ANOTHER EGG
by Harry Bliss
April 13, 1998
In the first sketch (left), the image seemed old-fashioned, evoking the typical commuter who appeared on New Yorker covers of the nineteen-seventies and eighties.

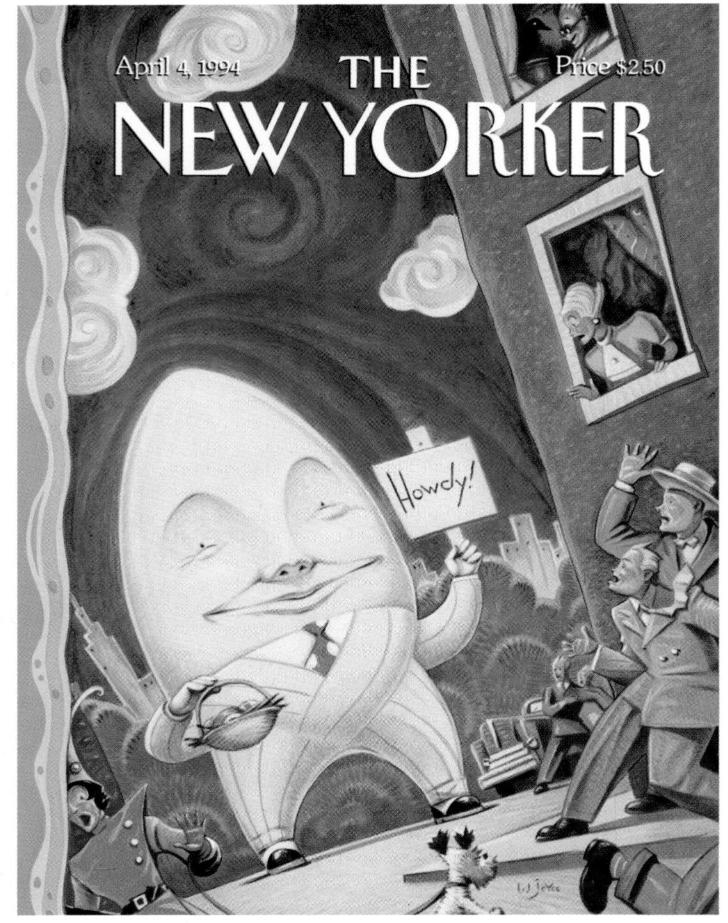

April 16, 1927
by Ilonka Karasz

PARADE BEST by Maira Kalman
April 8, 1996

TAXES

Sometimes a seemingly mundane topic inspires great covers.

left:
MARCH 15, 1947
by Constantin Alajálov

below, left:
MARCH 15, 1941
by Constantin Alajálov

below, right:
NOTHING IS CERTAIN BUT...
by Istvan Banyai
April 20, 1998

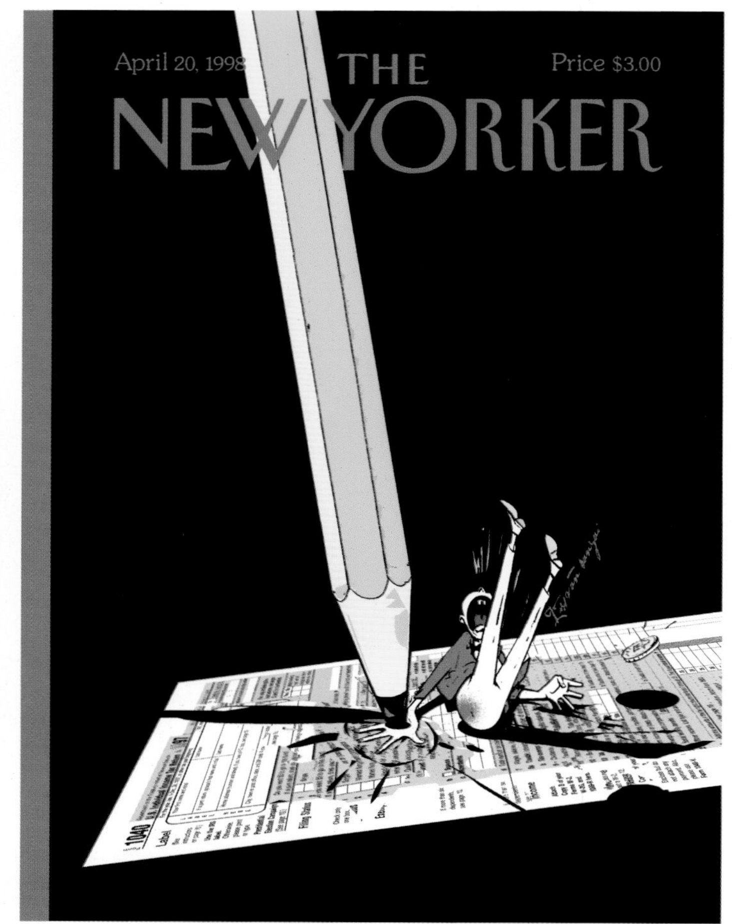

Shakedown by Richard McGuire
April 15, 1996

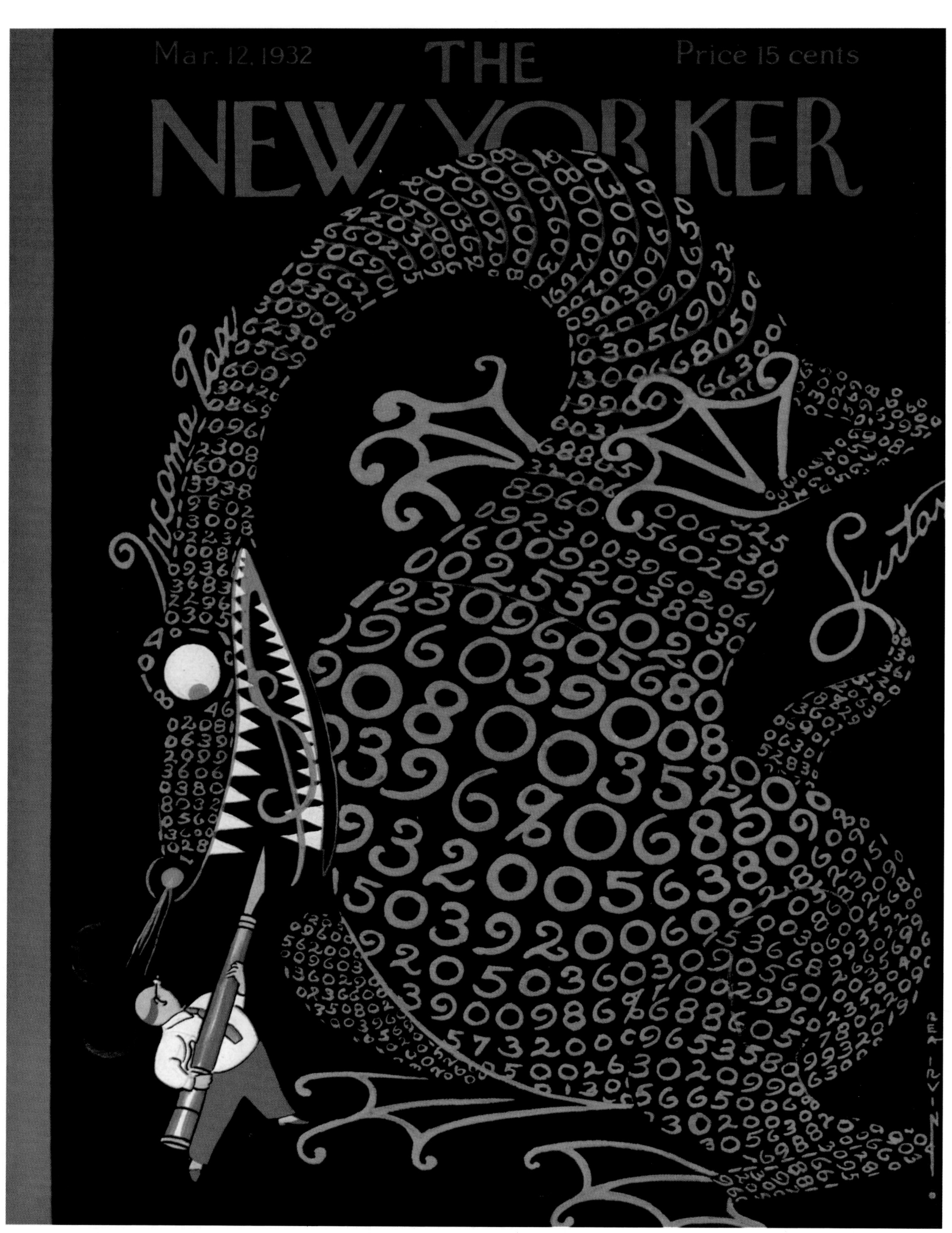

MARCH 12, 1932
by Rea Irvin
In the thirties, tax returns were due by March 15th.

MARCH 5, 1938
by Constantin Alajálov

MOTHER'S DAY

left:
MOMS
by Edward Sorel
May 9, 1994

below, left:
MOTHER'S DAY
by HA (Bob Zoell)
May 15, 1995

below, right:
LUNCH BREAKS
by Art Spiegelman
May 11, 1998

opposite:
HERE'S TO YOU, MOM
by Harry Bliss
May 10, 1999

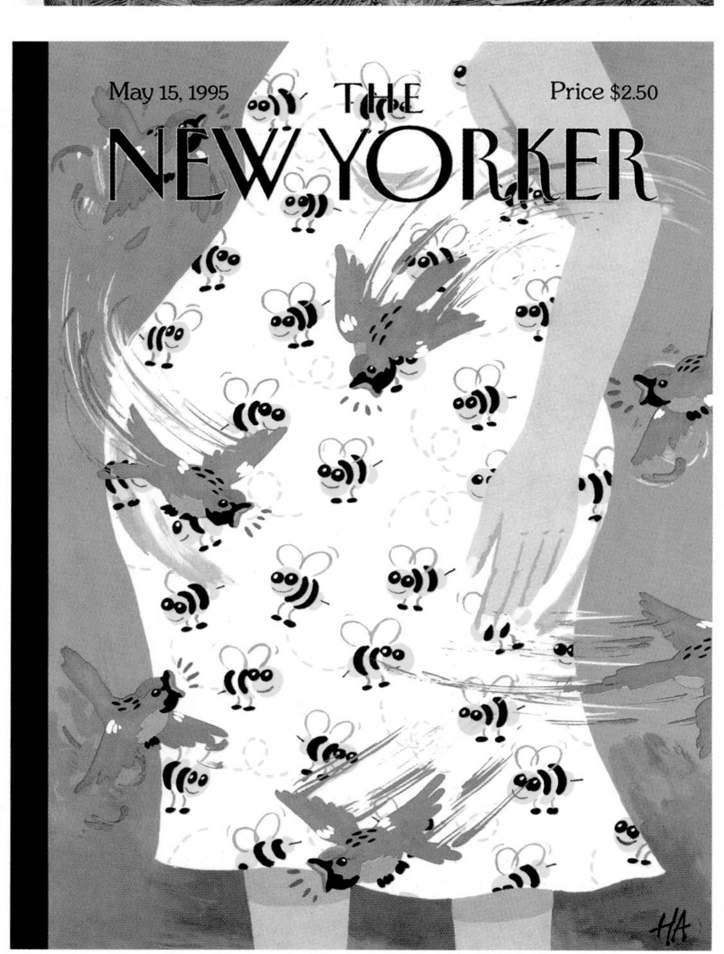

MOM

opposite:
MOTHER NATURE by Carter Goodrich
May 15, 2000

MAY 20, 1939
by Leonard Dove

MOTHER'S DAY by Ian Falconer
May 12, 1997
A sixty-three-year-old woman had recently given birth when this cover ran.

WAITING by Edward Sorel
May 13, 1996

WEDDINGS

right:
JUNE 11, 1927
by Rea Irvin

below, left:
MODERN MARRIAGE
by George Riemann
June 9, 1997

below, right:
AND FORSAKING ALL OTHERS
by Edward Sorel
June 15, 1998

opposite:

Although Jacques de Loustal used the traditional pose of a bride and groom, he attempted to avoid type-casting. Part of the solution was to make the man dressed in white taller than his partner.

JUNE GROOMS by Jacques de Loustal
June 13, 1994

THE ICING ON THE CAKE by Ian Falconer
June 7, 1999
A toast to the trophy wife. Her thirties equivalent would more likely have been a mistress than a bride.

JUNE 29, 1940
by Mary Petty

GRADUATION

right:
JUNE 9, 1934
by Helen E. Hokinson

below, left:
JUNE 13, 1936
by Leonard Dove

The cigarette and the mortarboard identify this sophisticate as a thoroughly modern woman.

below, right:
WAITING AROUND AFTER SCHOOL
by Barry Blitt
June 1, 1998

opposite:
GRADUATION
by M. Scott Miller
June 2, 1997

JUNE 22, 1935
by Constantin Alajálov

CLASSIFIEDS OF '96 by Art Spiegelman
May 20, 1996

WM JOYCE
I ♥ DAD

FATHER'S DAY

opposite:
FATHER'S DAY
by William Joyce
June 12, 2000

William Joyce's own son inspired this illustration of how a child upends his parents' working lives.

above, left:
JUNE 21, 1969
by Charles Saxon

above, right:
FATHER'S DAY
by Kathy Osborn
June 19, 1995

right:
FATHER'S DAY
by HA (Bob Zoell)
June 20, 1994

INDEPENDENCE DAY

left:
JULY 5, 1941
by James Thurber

below, left:
UNEXPECTED SURPLUS
by Edward Sorel
July 6, 1998

below, right:
FIREWORKS
by R. Sikoryak
July 7, 1997

This cover ran around the time that Congress was once again debating a constitutional amendment banning the burning of the American flag.

opposite:
INDEPENDENCE DAY
by Harry Bliss
July 5, 1999

pages 140 and 141:

Two of the seven covers William Steig drew over the years on the subject of firecrackers.

Price $3.00

THE NEW YORKER

July 5, 1999

JULY 3, 1937
by William Steig

JULY 5, 1982
by William Steig

McGUIRE

SUMMER

opposite:
HOT TOWN
by Richard McGuire
August 15, 1994

left:
MANNAHATTA RISING
by Lorenzo Mattotti
June 21, 1993

below, left:
JULY 8, 1933
by Will Cotton

below, right:
AT THE BEACH
by Charles Burns
July 29, 1996

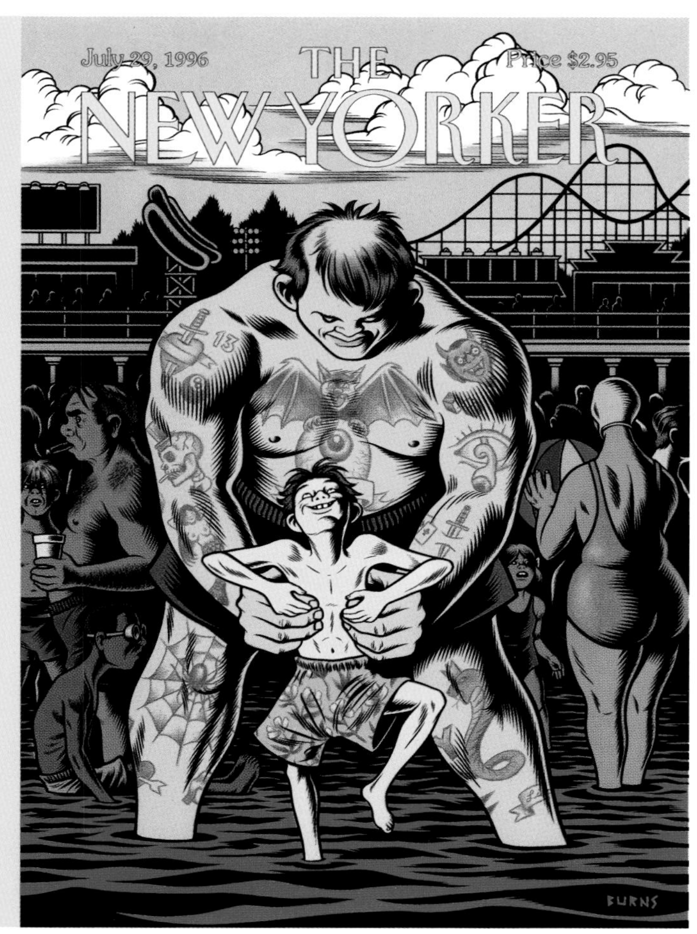

left:

YEARNING TO BREAK FREE
by Denis Roche
August 18, 1997

The artist did many different finished versions of this image, but we ended up using the original sketch, as it was the liveliest.

below, left:

THE BIG SPLASH
by Mark Ulriksen
July 11, 1994

below, right:

LIBERTY
by Peter de Sève
May 25, 1998

THE OCEAN OR BUST by Mariscal
August 9, 1993
In summer, New Yorker covers often leave the city behind.

right:
How to Swim
by Benoît van Innis
August 2, 1993

below, left:
Hot Enough for You?
by Richard McGuire
July 26, 1999

below, right:
Loft Life
by Mariscal
August 1, 1994

opposite:
Lobsterman's Special
by Bruce McCall
August 4, 1997

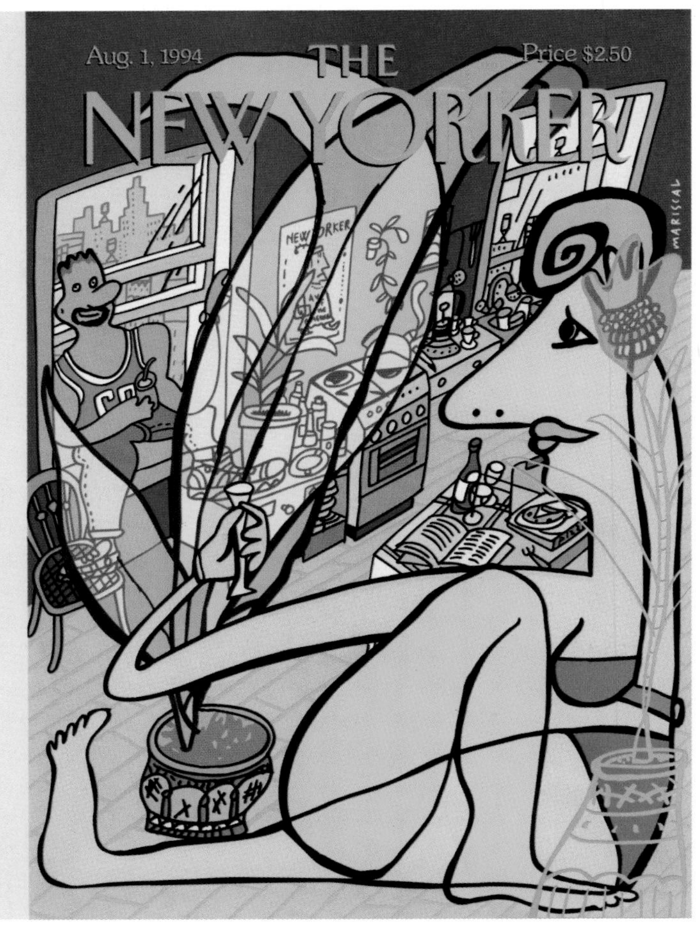

BRUCE McCALL

HEAT WAVE by Michael Roberts
August 9, 1999

DIVING IN by Lorenzo Mattotti
August 21 & 28, 1995

sempé.

opposite:
LES PIEDS SUR TERRE
by J. J. Sempé
August 11, 1997

right:
PICASSO ON THE BEACH
by Tom Hachtman
August 8, 1994

below, left:
MEMORIAL DAY
by Mark Zingarelli
June 6, 1994

below, right:
GETTING AWAY FROM IT ALL
by Ian Falconer
July 14, 1997

JULY 8, 1939
by Richard Taylor

HIGHER CALLING by Carter Goodrich
August 3, 1998

SUMMER TERRACE by Mariscal
August 7, 1995

BLOCK ISLAND WEEKEND by Gretchen Dow Simpson
June 7, 1993

above:

Sketches by Bruce McCall as he searched for the optimal point of view for "Welcome to Hellhampton" (opposite).

left:

LABOR DAY
by Peter de Sève
September 5, 1994

below:

LABOR DAY
by Peter de Sève
September 6, 1993

WELCOME TO HELLHAMPTON by Bruce McCall
September 6, 1999

BACK TO SCHOOL

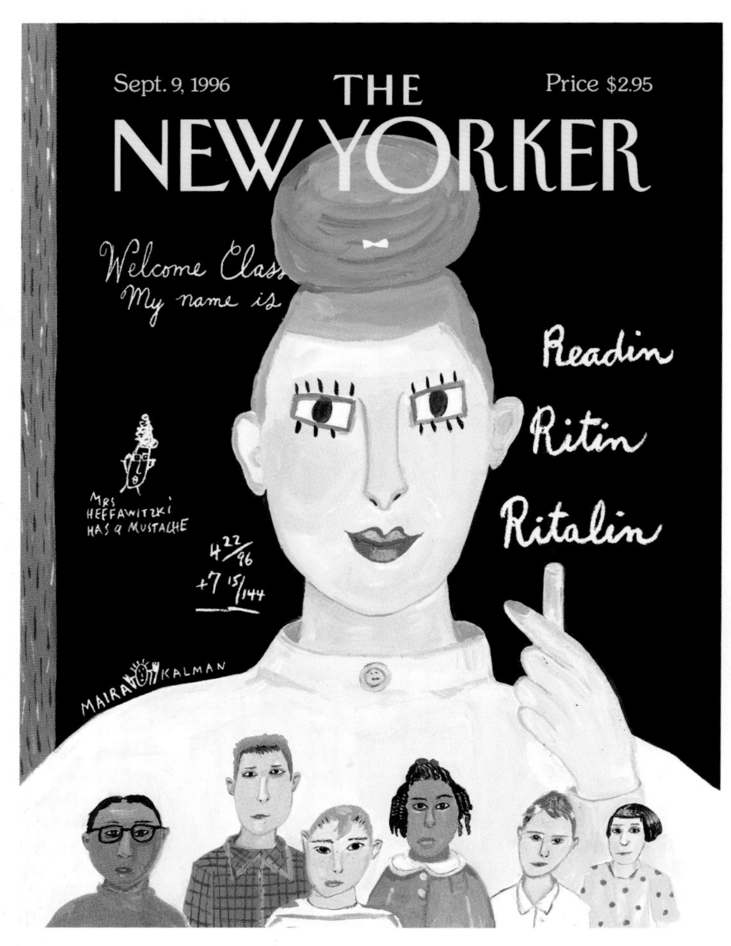

left:
THE THREE R'S
by Maira Kalman
September 9, 1996
and two preliminary sketches

below, left:
SEPTEMBER 6, 1969
by James Stevenson
This is one of the few covers where the artist played with the logo.

below, right:
NEWS R US
by Art Spiegelman
September 11, 1995

opposite:
BRACE YOURSELF
by Owen Smith
September 13, 1999
After the killings at Columbine High, there were demands for metal detectors in schools across the country.

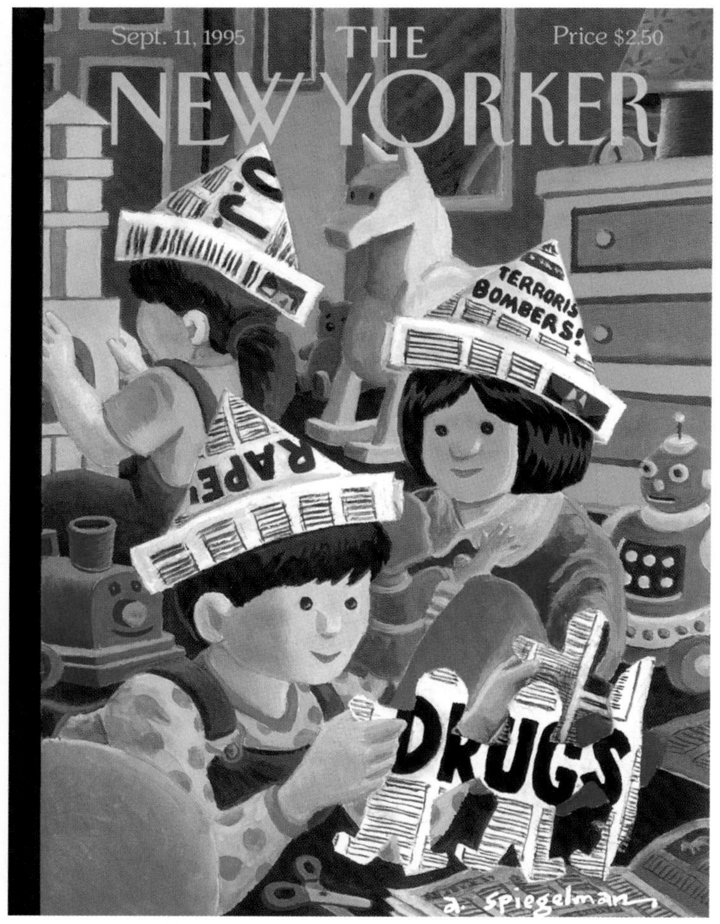

SCHOOL SECURITY
O Smith

BACK TO SCHOOL by William Joyce
September 14, 1998

THE GUNS OF SEPTEMBER by Art Spiegelman
September 13, 1993
Since 1993, several groups lobbying for gun control have asked for permission to use this image.

FALL

above, far left:
NOVEMBER 27, 1926
by Peter Arno
Peter Arno's first cover.

above, left:
APRIL 9, 1927
by Peter Arno
Arno's second cover.

left:
OCTOBER 29, 1938
by Peter Arno

opposite:
FALL GUISE
by Michael Roberts
November 10, 1997

MR

left:
FALL COLORS
by Edward Sorel
October 13, 1997

below, left:
FALL
by David Mazzucchelli
October 24, 1994

below, right:
THE FALL
by Edward Sorel
October 3, 1994

THE FALL by J. J. Sempé
November 15, 1999

THE DELUGE by Edward Sorel
October 7, 1996

REMEMBRANCE OF FLINGS PAST by Edward Sorel
October 4, 1993

HALLOWEEN

clockwise from right:
STRANGE BREW
by Charles Burns
November 1, 1993

NOVEMBER 4, 1985
by George Booth

HELL ON WHEELS
by Edward Sorel
October 30, 1995

opposite:
OCTOBER 31, 1942
by Rea Irvin

Oct. 31, 1942

THE NEW YORKER

Price 15 cents

W.Joyce

opposite:
HALLOWEEN
by William Joyce
October 31, 1994

left:
OCTOBER 30, 1989
by Charles Addams
Addams's last cover.

below, left:
TREATS OF THE TRADE
by Harry Bliss
November 1, 1999

below, right:
OCTOBER 31, 1983
by Charles Addams

THANKSGIVING

clockwise from right:
THANKSGIVING
by Kathy Osborn
November 28, 1994

TURKEY SHOOT
by Ian Falconer
December 1, 1997

NOVEMBER 26, 1938
by Will Cotton

opposite, clockwise from top left:
NOVEMBER 27, 1978
by Charles Addams

TURKEY DAY
by Steve Brodner
November 29, 1999

DRESSED TURKEY
by Peter de Sève
December 2, 1996

GUESS WHO'S COMING TO DINNER
by Benoît van Innis
November 29, 1993

Nov.27,1978
THE NEW YORKER
One Dollar

Price $3.00
THE NEW YORKER
Nov. 29, 1999

Nov. 29, 1993
THE NEW YORKER
Price $1.95
BENOÎT

Dec. 2, 1996
THE NEW YORKER
Price $2.95

opposite:
MOUSE AMOK by William Joyce
November 27, 1995

NOVEMBER 24, 1934
by Will Cotton

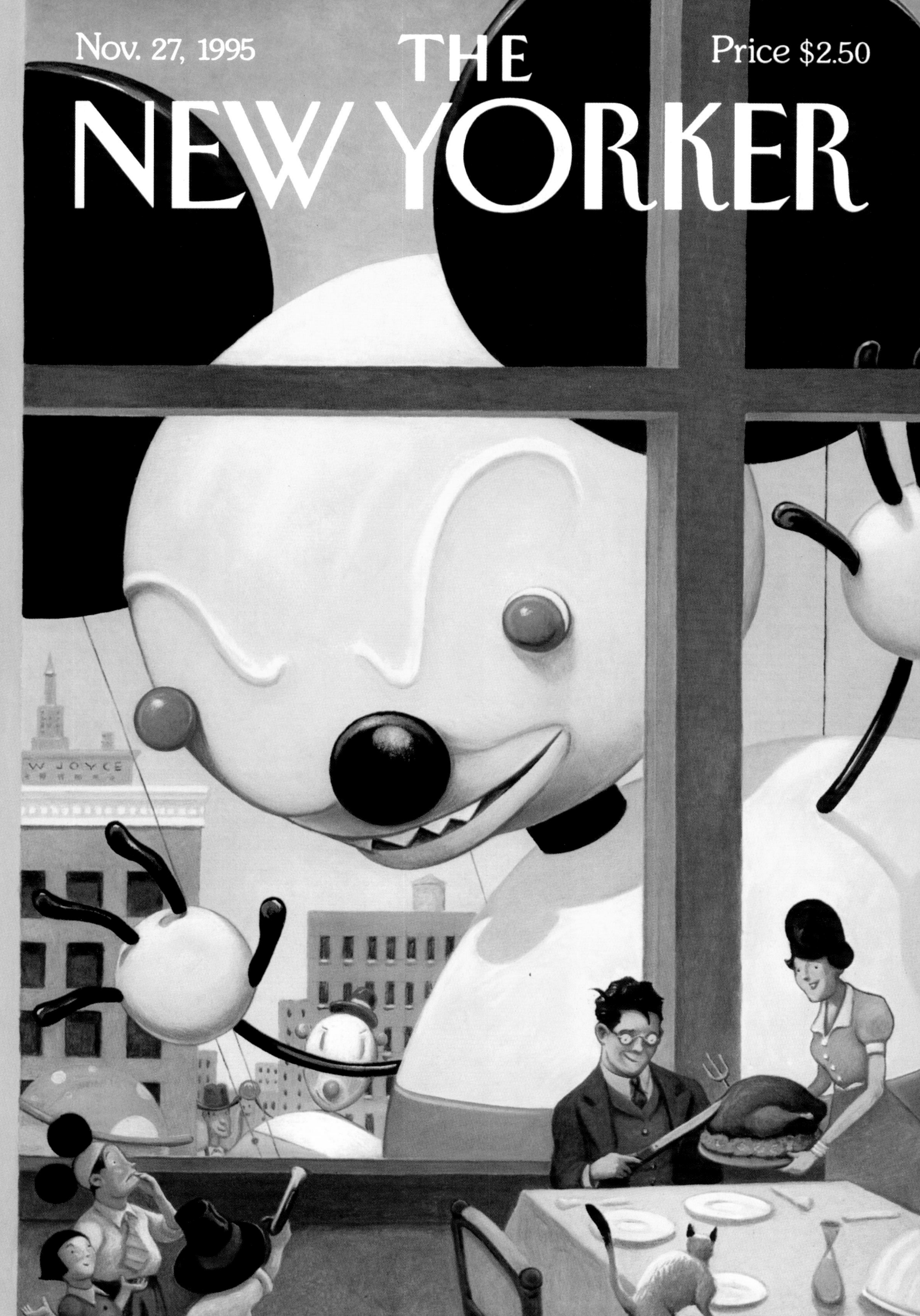
Nov. 27, 1995
THE NEW YORKER
Price $2.50
W JOYCE

CHRISTMAS

left:
ALL LIT UP
by J. J. Sempé
December 20, 1993

below, left:
PRE-HOLIDAY RUSH
by Ever Meulen
December 5, 1994

below, right:
DECEMBER 25, 1965
by George Price

opposite:
SANTA CITY
by Max
December 18, 1995

clockwise from right:
DECEMBER 14, 1992
by Michael Witte

DECEMBER 11, 1948
by Will Cotton

THE BIG BAG
by Franco Matticchio
December 13, 1999

opposite, clockwise from top left:
HOLIDAY TRAFFIC
by Carter Goodrich
December 19, 1994

CHRISTMAS PAST,
CHRISTMAS PRESENT
by Edward Sorel
December 16, 1996

CHRISTMAS DECORATIONS
by Benoît van Innis
December 21, 1998

INSTALLATION
by Benoît van Innis
December 20, 1999

Dec. 19, 1994
THE
NEW YORKER
Price $2.50

Dec. 16, 1996
THE
NEW YORKER
Price $2.95
EDWARD SOREL

Price $3.00
THE
NEW YORKER
Dec. 20, 1999
BENOÎT

Price $3.00
THE
NEW YORKER
Dec. 21, 1998
BENOÎT

opposite:
DECEMBER 20, 1958
by Peter Arno

SANTA CLAUS IN TOWN by William Joyce
December 12, 1994

Falconer

THE ARTS

DECEMBER 8, 1928
by Peter Arno

opposite:
ART APPRECIATION by Ian Falconer
November 23, 1998

THE ART WORLD

counterclockwise from left:

MIRÓ IN THE CITY
by Mariscal
November 15, 1993

Mariscal is one of the most interesting and lively artists working in Barcelona. This cover pays homage to his hero, Joan Miró, who was having a show at the Museum of Modern Art in New York.

CAVE OPENING
by Harry Bliss
March 15, 1999

After this cover ran, Harry Bliss got a call from a magazine specializing in paleontology and archeology, and he's been a staff cartoonist there ever since.

THE PLASTIC ARTS
by Art Spiegelman
April 19, 1999

Spiegelman's profile of the cartoonist Jack Cole, creator of the comic-strip superhero Plastic Man, ran, together with this cover, during a Picasso show at the Guggenheim Museum.

Two treatments of the same subject.

below:

JANUARY 15, 1955
by Charles E. Martin

opposite:

Cotton's masterly composition enhances storytelling: the curve of the woman's body is set against the verticals of the guard, the walls, and the frames of the paintings, and contrasted with the thrust of the sculpture.

SEPTEMBER 19, 1936
by Will Cotton

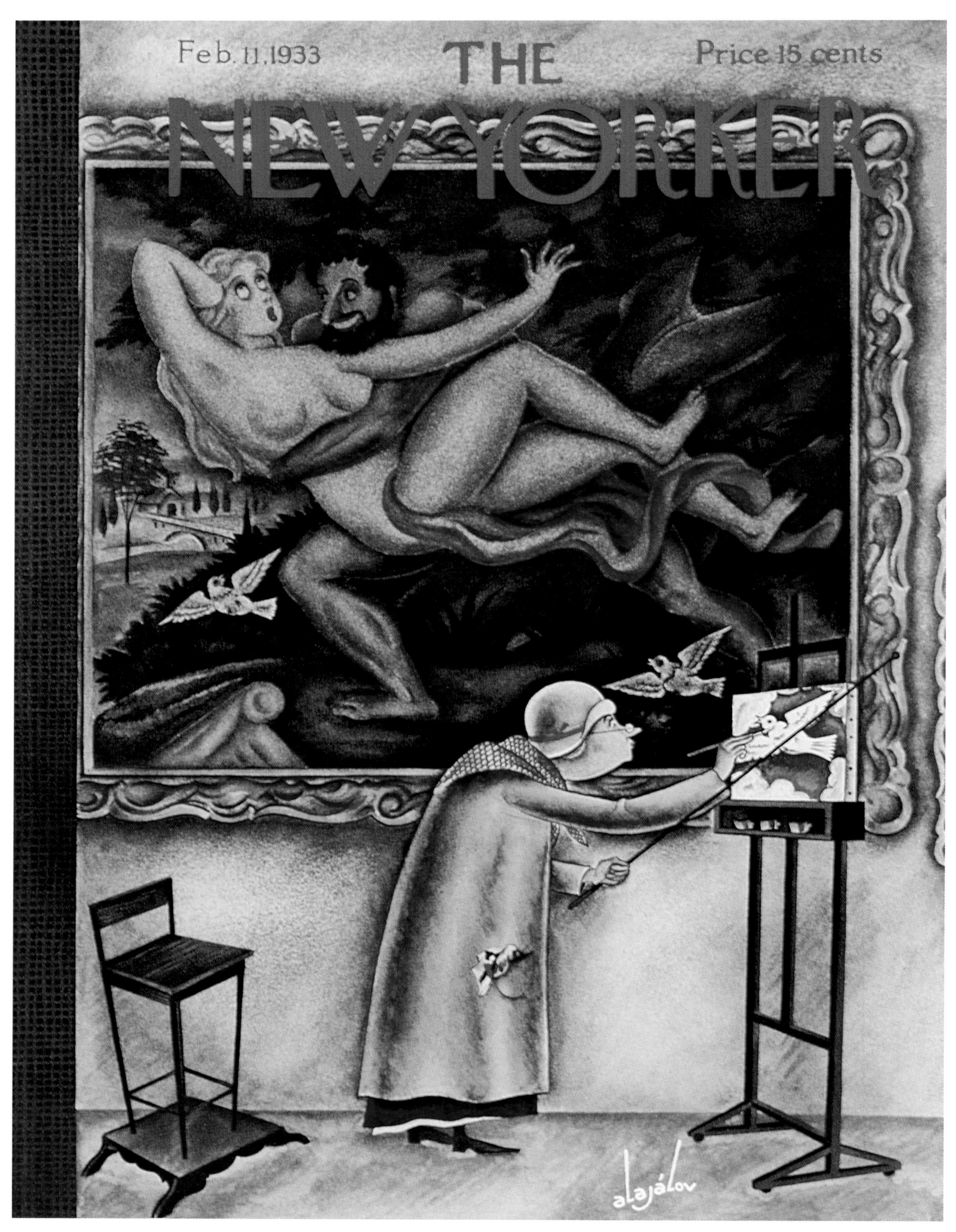

FEBRUARY 11, 1933
by Constantin Alajálov
Puritanism about the arts was around . . .

OPEN-MINDED MAYOR by Art Spiegelman
October 11, 1999
. . . even before Mayor Rudolph Giuliani had to confront the "Sensation" show at the Brooklyn Museum of Art.

BOOKS & FICTION ISSUES

counterclockwise from left:

THE UNBEARABLE LIGHTNESS OF READING
by Ever Meulen
October 4, 1999

FALL BOOKS
by Joost Swarte
October 5, 1998

TALL STORIES
by Max
October 6, 1997

opposite, clockwise from top left:

THE MELTING PLOT
by Edward Sorel
June 27 & July 4, 1994

WINTER FICTION
by Art Spiegelman
December 28, 1998 & January 4, 1999

THE ELEPHANTINE PROPHECY
by Owen Smith
June 23 & 30, 1997

20 WRITERS FOR THE 21ST CENTURY
by Chip Kidd and Chris Ware
June 21 & 28, 1999

Price $3.95 THE June 21 & 28, 1999

NEW YORKER

1. Being a Spokane Indian, I only pick up Indian hitchhikers. I learned this particular ceremony from my father, a
2. Lee Strasberg, a founder of the Group Theatre and the great teacher of the American Method, famously advised
3. The autumn I was seventeen Richard Nixon made a visit to our town, at the western edge of Cape Cod, and I we
4. Josef Kavalier's determination to storm the exclusive Hofzinser Club of Prague took full form over breakfast one
5. My father is gone. I am slouched in a cast-aluminum chair across from two men, one the manager of the hotel D
6. He sits on the mattress, the fat spread of his ass popping my fitted sheets from their corners. His clothes are stiff fr
7. Jim and Uncle Al did not set out on their journey until after supper, when the heat of the day had broken at last,
8. Allen Fein is on his way to Port Authority when he stubs his toe and scuffs his shoe—puts a nick in a five-hundre
9. Skulls make better pillows than you think. Dr. Peter Luce (the famous sexologist) rests his cheek on the varnishe
10. Down the long concourse they came unsteadily, Enid favoring her damaged hip, Alfred paddling at the air with un
11. You couldn't tell anymore that they had separate desks. For fifteen years, Roselva and Helen had worked togethe
12. on a raft in water. Floating. Every day when she comes home from school, she puts on her bikini and
13. ppy East Coast resort island in the middle of summer, we just flew in for the wedding of my incre
14. with a certificate in commerce and the equivalent, in those days, of ten dollars to my name. Fo
15. man, I didn't seek out the pleasure of women. At least not like my comrades in arms, who i
16. reamers, by the bathhouse entrance. Tuna on shish kebab and pineapple slices in lar
17. l Emily. She caught her breath. Everything was striking her in the solar plexus
18. letter of 23 Feb., which accompanied the I CAN SPEAK!™ you returned, much
19. -haired, pale-faced, slender idealist, tells itself with a grim brevity, in keeping
20. t as a asset like that would you. But it's the arm. You want to see it? You wo

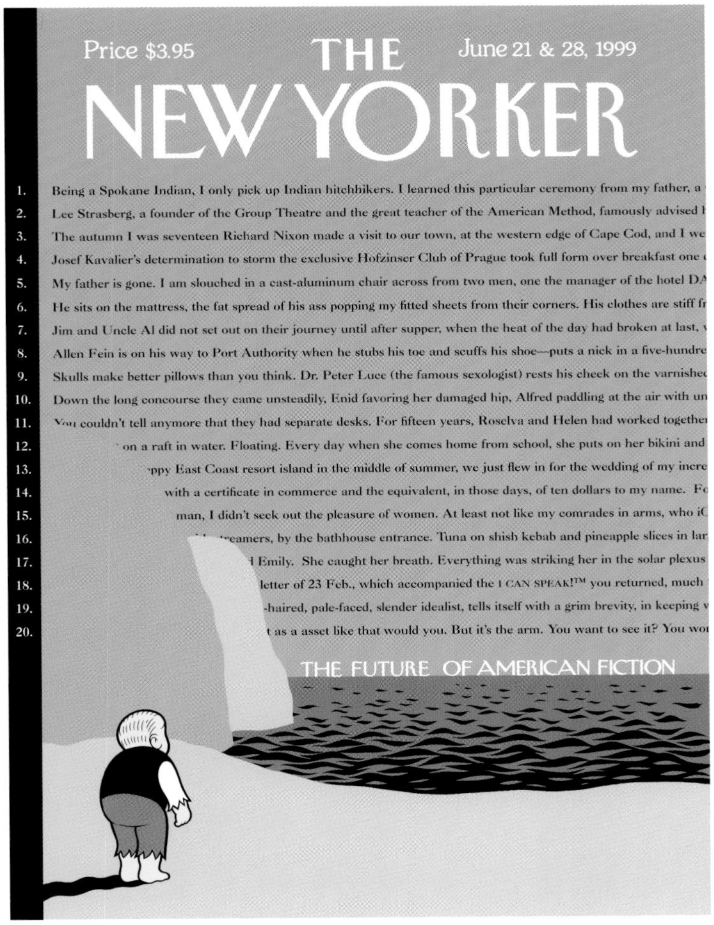

THE FUTURE OF AMERICAN FICTION

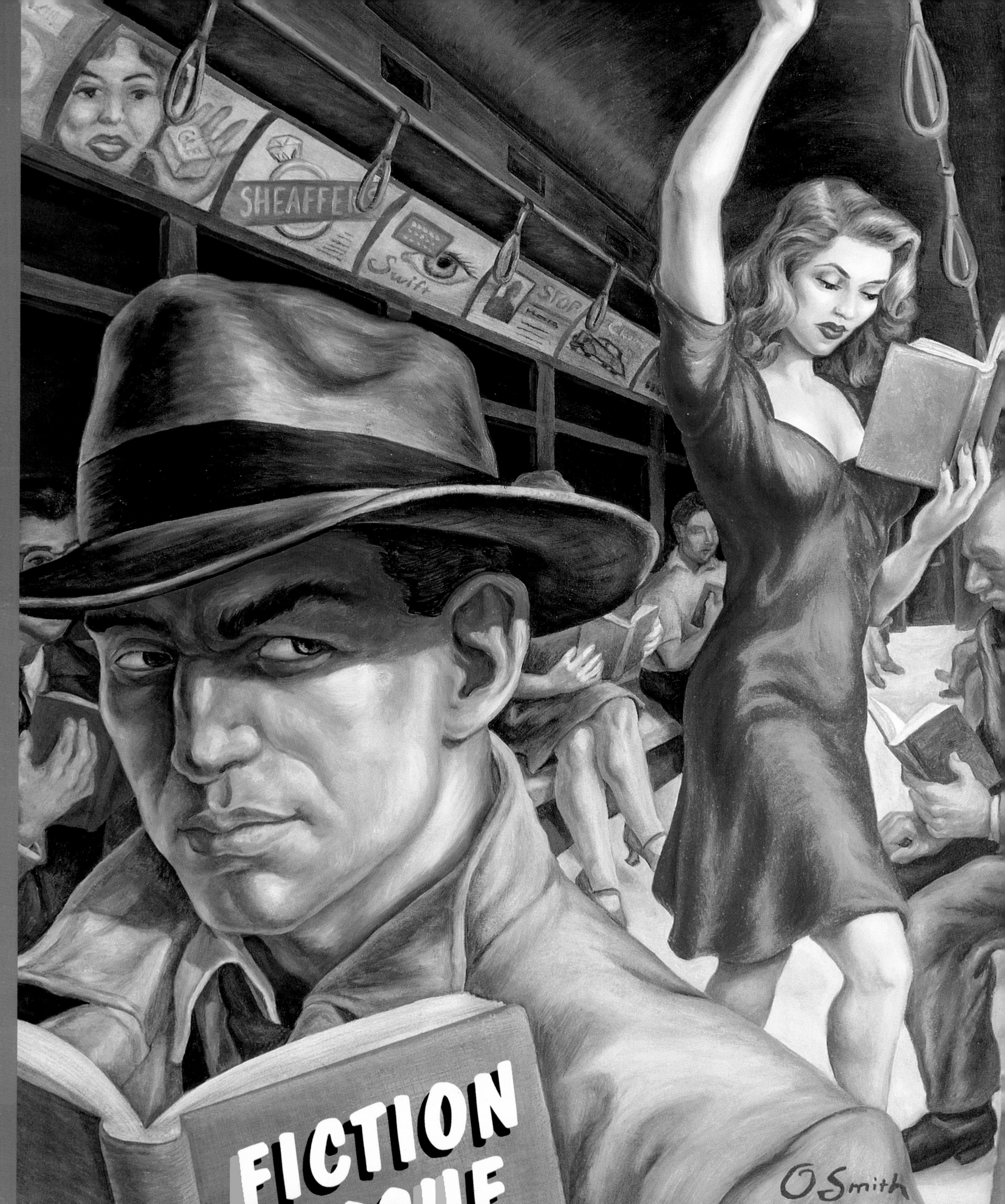
Swift
STOP
FICTION
O.Smith

opposite:

PAPERBACK RIDERS
by Owen Smith
June 26 & July 3, 1995

clockwise from above, left, all by Owen Smith:

THE WRITING LIFE
December 25, 1995 & January 1, 1996

BEDSIDE STORIES
December 23 & 30, 1996

A CREATURE WAS STIRRING
December 22 & 29, 1997

TUNNEL OF LOVE
June 24 & July 1, 1996

BEACH READING
June 22 & 29, 1998

THE MOVIES

left:

STARRY NIGHT
by Edward Sorel
March 29, 1993

below, left:

A NIGHT TO REMEMBER
by Art Spiegelman
March 23, 1998

This was the year that James Cameron's "Titanic" swamped the Oscars.

below, right:

MOVIE NUMBER
by Edward Sorel
March 21, 1994

opposite:

OSCAR CLOSEUP
by Lorenzo Mattotti
March 27, 1995

counterclockwise from left:

"CUT!"
by Bruce McCall
December 8, 1997

A NIGHT AT THE MOVIES
by Roxie Munro
March 8, 1993

OFF TO SEE THE WIZARD
by Barry Blitt
November 16, 1998

CALL 911-FILM
by Art Spiegelman
May 26, 1997

opposite:

THE MOMENT OF TRUTH
by Carter Goodrich
March 25, 1996

Making one square slightly bigger than the others captures the moment the image of the Oscar winner gets bigger on the TV screen. Some of the people here are identifiable actors—Jack Nicholson, for example—but the four main characters are anonymous. Caricaturing both recognizable and generic faces in the same image is a remarkable accomplishment.

Price $3.00
THE
Nov. 16, 1998
NEW YORKER

JULY 8, 1961
by Charles Addams

JURASSIC PERKS by Edward Sorel
June 14, 1993

FASHION

left:

FASHION WEEK
by Lorenzo Mattotti
November 6, 1995

Many of New York's fashion shows that fall took place in a tent in the newly renovated Bryant Park.

below, left:

AUGUST 10, 1992
by Edward Koren

below, right:

NIGHT LIFE
by Lorenzo Mattotti
April 10, 2000

opposite:

VIVIENNE WESTWOOD, PARIS PRÊT-À-PORTER
by Lorenzo Mattotti
November 8, 1993

Nov. 8, 1993
THE
NEW YORKER
Price $1.95

Mar. 17, 1997
THE
NEW YORKER
Price $2.95
MR

opposite:
CHEEP CHIC
by Michael Roberts
March 17, 1997

clockwise from right, all by Michael Roberts:
STEELING BEAUTY
September 20, 1999

BELOW THE BELT
July 28, 1997

DROP-DEAD CHIC
March 30, 1998

SPOT CHECK
September 21, 1998

below:
APRIL 17, 1926
by Clayton Knight

right:
MARCH 18, 1939
by Barbara Shermund

below, left:
THE LOOK
by Robert Risko
February 7, 1994

The anorexic look was then so pervasive in fashion that models seemed almost like clothes hangers.

below, right:
MAY 10, 1941
by Constantin Alajálov

opposite:
This was one of our first special fashion issues. In addition to the Spiegelman cover, it had a portfolio of fashion drawings by Lorenzo Mattotti and an artist-at-large piece by Sue Coe about sweatshops in New York City.

UNVEILED by Art Spiegelman
November 7, 1994

THEATRE

right:
NOVEMBER 5, 1927
by Constantin Alajálov

below, left:
THE THRILL OF THE THEATRE
by Ian Falconer
June 8, 1998

below, right:
MARCH 26, 1949
by Constantin Alajálov

Constantin Alajálov was a prolific Russian émigré painter and illustrator who did covers for The New Yorker, as well as for Vanity Fair and other magazines, starting in the nineteen-twenties. His style evolved quickly to include a masterly use of various elements (such as the timetable at the left) in visual storytelling.

opposite:
APRIL 3, 1948
by Constantin Alajálov

alajálov.

OPERA

left:

NOVEMBER 16, 1992
by Arnold Roth

below, left:

DOUBLEHEADER
by Harry Bliss
October 19, 1998

At the time, the Yankees were in the World Series.

below, right:

JANUARY 7, 1928
by Constantin Alajálov

OPENING NIGHT by Edward Sorel
September 29, 1997

MUSIC AND DANCE

left:

JANUARY 26, 1929
by Rea Irvin

far left:

JANUARY 22, 1979
by J. J. Sempé

Two music lessons, by Irvin and Sempé, almost exactly fifty years apart.

left:

OCTOBER 24, 1931
by Rose Silver

below:

JANUARY 6, 1940
by Peter Arno

PLUGGED IN by Ceesepe
November 22, 1993

Music hall, cabaret, blues, and the essence of jazz.

right:
OCTOBER 17, 1925
by Max Rée

below, left:
DECEMBER 3, 1927
by Constantin Alajálov

below, right:
HEAVENLY BLUES
by Carter Goodrich
December 11, 1995

opposite:
FEBRUARY 6, 1926
by Vladimir Bobritsky

BOBRITSKY

JANUARY 28, 1985
by J. J. Sempé

MARCH 12, 1984
by J. J. Sempé

J. J. SEMPÉ

Jean-Jacques Sempé has not taken well to faxes, FedExes or E-mails, and it is a pleasure to visit him in his Paris studio two or three times a year and look at drawings that he has put aside for *The New Yorker.* He was first published in the magazine under Shawn, in the nineteen-seventies, and it was a delight for me to find him here. Sempé is quite well known in France, and I had grown up with his books; in fact, it would surprise many of my compatriots to see how well he is able to capture New York, since they think of his work as classically French. His characters' facial expressions are exquisitely drawn, and are just one element of the nuanced humanity of his compositions. Combining masterly storytelling with artful rendering, Sempé is undoubtedly a quintessential *New Yorker* cover artist.

DECEMBER 12, 1988
by J. J. Sempé

BALLET'S NEW SPRING by J. J. Sempé
May 3, 1993

ARABESQUE by J. J. Sempé
September 20, 1993

left:
MARCH 9, 1981
by J. J. Sempé

below, left:
SLIGHT ANXIETY
by J. J. Sempé
March 29, 1999

below, right:
JANUARY 5, 1987
by J. J. Sempé

opposite:
THE BOY WHO WANTED TO BE PRESIDENT
by J. J. Sempé
February 5, 1996

Sempé

84
Merkin

SPORTS

MAY 23, 1988
by Charles Addams

APRIL 5, 1993
by Richard Merkin

left:
THE LAST JUDGMENT
by Edward Sorel
September 4, 1995

below, left:
SEPTEMBER 5, 1925
by Jimmie the Ink
(James H. Daugherty)

below, right:
JUNE 19, 1971
by Charles Saxon

opposite, clockwise from top left:
PLAY BALL!
by Mark Ulriksen
May 1, 1995

THE FIRST PITCH
by Arnold Roth
April 3, 2000

HUDDLE
by Mark Ulriksen
October 17, 1994

OCTOBER 28, 1939
by Constantin Alajálov

May 1, 1995
THE
NEW YORKER
Price $2.50

PRICE $3.00
THE
NEW YORKER
APRIL 3, 2000

Oct. 28, 1939
THE
NEW YORKER
Price 15 cents

Oct. 17, 1994
THE
NEW YORKER
Price $2.50

left:
COUPE DU MONDE
by Ana Juan
July 13, 1998

below, left:
TOO BUSY CITY
by William Joyce
July 22, 1996

below, right:
FIGURE-SKATING FAN
by Mark Ulriksen
February 9, 1998

page 224:
MAY 8, 1926
by Vladimir Bobritsky

page 225:
OPENING DAY
by Mark Ulriksen
April 12, 1999

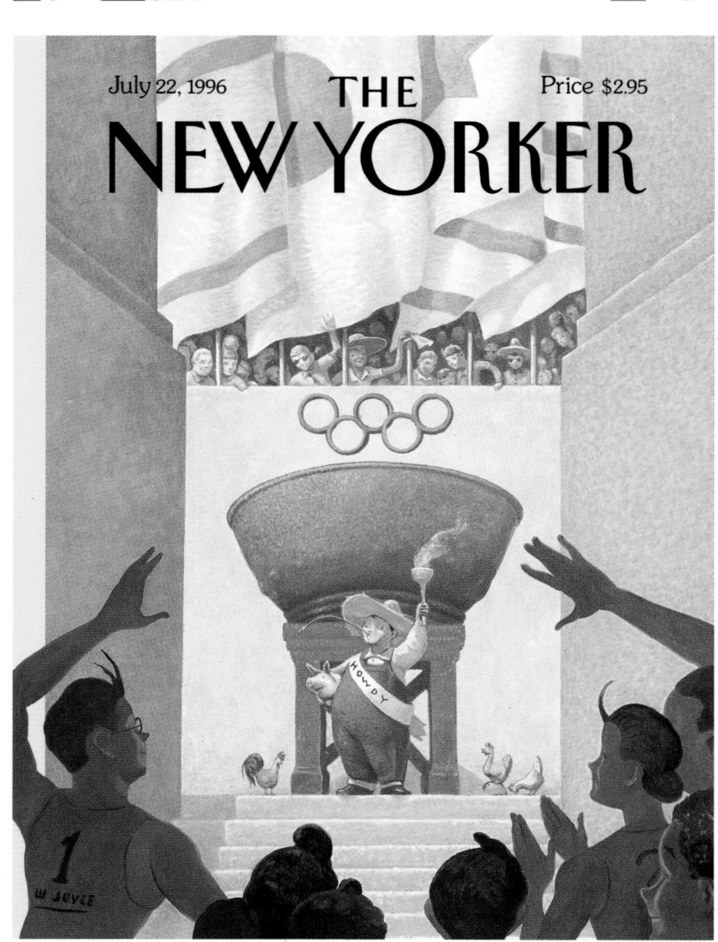

TOUR DE FRANCE by J. J. Sempé
July 12, 1999

BORRITSKY

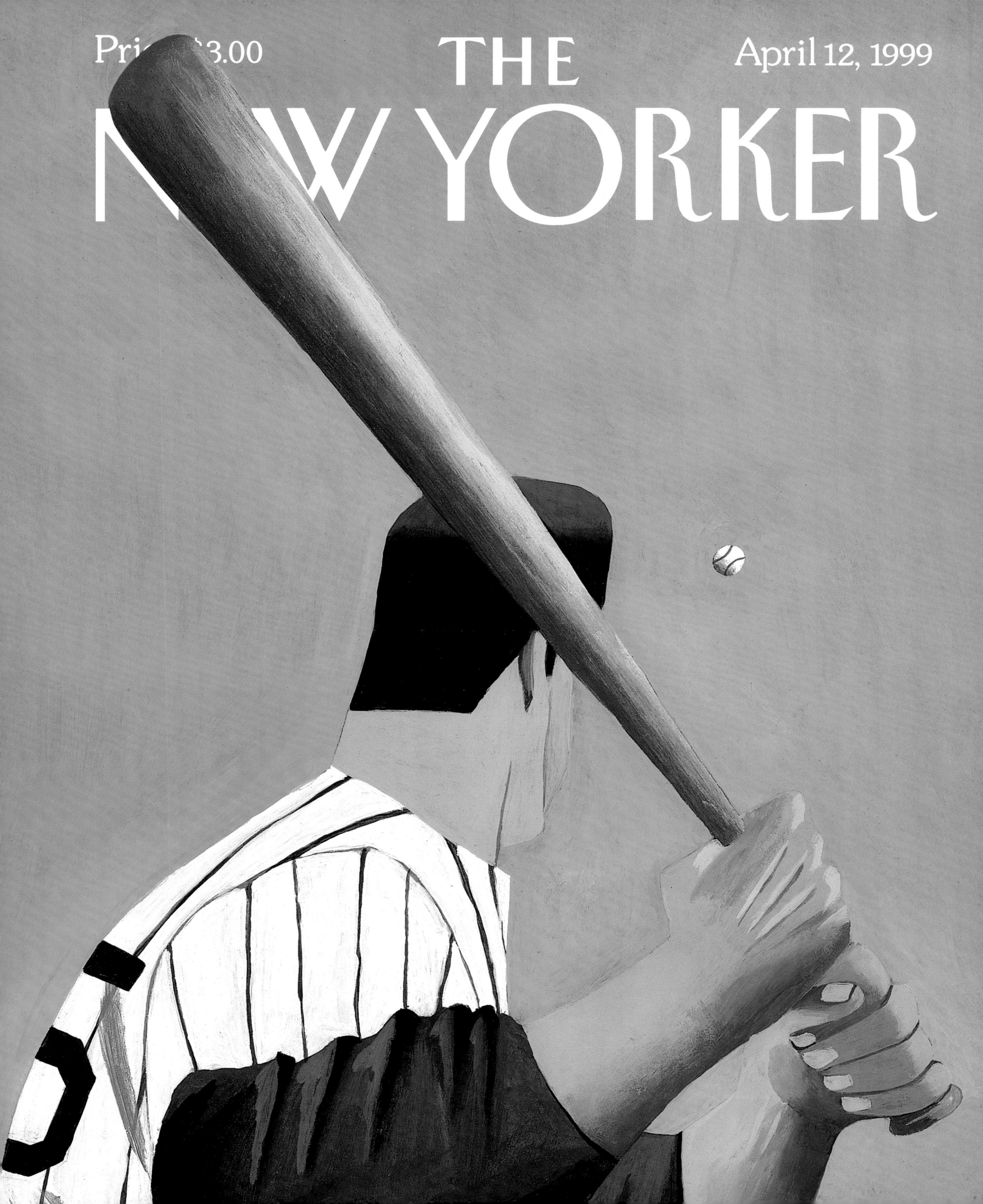

Price $3.00
THE
NEW YORKER
April 12, 1999

PRICE $3.00 THE NEW YORKER MAR. 13, 2000

Falconer

TIME MARCHES ON by Ian Falconer
March 13, 2000

THE TIMELESS MOMENT

CAT
by Saul Steinberg
November 18, 1996

RED CARPET by J. J. Sempé
March 28, 1994

LUXURIOUS, QUIET, AND COZY by J. J. Sempé
November 24, 1997

NOVEMBER 23, 1968
by Saul Steinberg

FAMILY VALUES by Art Spiegelman
April 22, 1996

MAIN STREET
by Saul Steinberg, April 25, 1994

OCTOBER 20, 1975
by Saul Steinberg

SAUL STEINBERG

Steinberg may have been the most influential artist in *The New Yorker's* seventy-five years. He was a Romanian Jew studying architecture in Milan when, in 1940, a portfolio of his work, published in *Life*, came to the attention of Harold Ross and William Shawn. Despite filled immigration quotas, the magazine was able to sponsor a U.S. visa for him in 1942. Steinberg was also an eminent gallery artist—he was featured in a one-man show at the Whitney in 1978—but he was committed to doing images that could be published in magazines rather than seen only in art exhibitions. His father was a printer, and he loved printer's marks. Nothing pleased him more than to look at progressive color proofs and discuss whether to remove this line or that. His imprint was felt everywhere in the magazine, though he was perhaps even more in touch with its writers than with its artists.

opposite, bottom:
THE FIVE SENSES by Saul Steinberg
March 9, 1998

DECEMBER 4, 1971
by Saul Steinberg

FEBRUARY 5, 1972
by Saul Steinberg

WILSHIRE & LEX by Saul Steinberg
February 13, 1995

left:
OCTOBER 18, 1969
by Saul Steinberg

below, left:
LOOKING DOWN
by Saul Steinberg
February 28, 1994

below, right:
JANUARY 16, 1971
by Saul Steinberg

right:
MARCH 13, 1978
by Saul Steinberg

SEPTEMBER 20, 1976
by Saul Steinberg

SELECTIVE NEW YORKER TIME LINE

by Christopher Shay

FEB. 21, 1925 First issue of *The New Yorker,* with Eustace Tilley, as drawn by art editor Rea Irvin, on the cover. Irvin remains the art editor until 1939, and Tilley appears on the anniversary issue cover every February until 1994.

FEB. 28, 1925 Dorothy Parker's first contribution, the poem "Cassandra Drops Into Verse."

APR. 18, 1925 E. B. White's first short story, "A Step Forward."

OCT. 10, 1925 Janet Flanner's first Paris Letter.

FEB. 26, 1927 James Thurber's first byline, the poem "Villanelle of Horatio Street."

JUL. 23, 1927 Robert Benchley first writes on journalists; he continues The Wayward Press column until 1939.

MAY 25, 1929 S. N. Behrman's first published piece, a Profile of George Gershwin. Emily Hahn's first published piece, a short story, "Lovely Lady"; Hahn contributes fact and fiction until 1996.

JAN. 11, 1930 "Invocation," the first *New Yorker* poem by Ogden Nash.

DEC. 13, 1930 S. J. Perelman's story "Open Letter to Moira Ransom" is the first of more than 300 humor pieces he contributes. His last runs in 1979.

1931 First drawings by James Thurber.

James Thurber, Dec. 5, 1931

"Have you people got any .38 cartridges?"

NOV. 21, 1931 Lewis Mumford begins writing The Skyline architecture column, which he continues until 1963.

MAY 7, 1932 First cover by William Steig (still an active contributor), depicting a stern father analyzing his son's report card.

DEC. 24, 1932 Frank Sullivan begins a tradition with his first "Greetings, Friends" Christmas poem.

MAY 25, 1935 John Cheever's first short story, "Brooklyn Rooming House."

MAY 5, 1938 "Alumnae Bulletin," the first of 239 short stories by John H. O'Hara.

1939 James Geraghty replaces Rea Irvin as art editor. He remains art editor until 1973.

APR. 15, 1939 First poem by W. H. Auden, "Song."

APR. 11, 1942 Vladimir Nabokov's first contribution, a poem entitled "Literary Dinner."

1943 Size of the magazine changes from 8¾" x 11⅞" to 8½" x 11⅜", in response to wartime paper shortages.

JAN. 1, 1944 Edmund Wilson's first signed Books column.

MAY 19, 1945 A. J. Liebling begins writing The Wayward Press column.

AUG. 31, 1946 Entire issue is devoted to the 31,347-word Reporter at Large "Hiroshima," by John Hersey.

JUN. 26, 1948 Richard Wilbur's first poem, "Grasse: Olive Trees."

DECEMBER 6, 1951 Harold Ross dies.

JAN. 21, 1952 William Shawn becomes the editor.

MAY 17, 1952 V. S. Pritchett's first book review.

DEC. 5, 1953 Magazine devotes ninety-one pages to "The Ponder Heart," by Eudora Welty.

Charles Saxon, Dec. 28, 1957

"Why don't you admit it? All the time you're snarling at those drivers, it's me you're really snarling at."

OCT. 30, 1954 John Updike's first short story, "Friends from Philadelphia."

APR. 13, 1957 Whitney Balliett's first Jazz column.

MAY 4, 1957 "Zooey" by J.D. Salinger, at 41,000 words, is the longest piece of fiction to run in *The New Yorker.*

JUL. 12, 1958 Rea Irvin's last non-anniversary cover, showing a golfer looking for his lost ball.

DEC. 5, 1959 James Dickey's first poem, "Orpheus Before Hades."

APR. 7, 1962 Roger Angell's first Sporting Scene, on baseball.

JUN. 16–30, 1962 Rachel Carson's Reporter at Large, "Silent Spring," runs in three parts.

Lee Lorenz, Jun. 14, 1969

"Thank you, but I'm not looking for a contact lens. I'm crawling."

FEB. 16, 1963 First part of Hannah Arendt's three-part Reporter at Large "Eichmann in Jerusalem."

JUL. 13, 1963 Calvin Trillin's first signed piece, Reporter at Large on "An Education in Georgia."

SEPT. 19 & 26, 1964 Joseph Mitchell's last contribution, a two-part Profile of Joe Gould.

Ed Koren, Jul. 10, 1971

JAN. 23, 1965 John McPhee's first fact piece for the magazine, a Profile of the Princeton University basketball player William Warren Bradley.

SEPT. 25–OCT. 16, 1965 Truman Capote's "In Cold Blood" runs in four parts.

JAN. 22, 1966 Woody Allen's first humor piece, "The Gossage-Vardebedian Papers."

JUL. 15, 1967 Jonathan Schell's first piece, A Reporter at Large about a massacre in the Vietnamese village of Ben Suc.

JAN. 13, 1968 Pauline Kael's first movie review; first theatre review by the long-time contributor Brendan Gill.

MAR. 22, 1969 A complete table of contents—including titles, authors, and cartoonists—appears for the first time.

1973 With the retirement of James Geraghty, Lee Lorenz, a cartoonist since 1958, becomes art editor.

JUL. 2, 1973 Beginning with this issue, *The New Yorker* is dated on Mondays instead of on Saturdays.

James Stevenson, Jan. 11, 1988

"My day? One amazing slam-dunk after another."

JUL. 12, 1976 Veronica Geng's first casual, "More Mathematical Puzzles & Diversions."

MAR. 14, 1977 Alice Munro's first short story, "Royal Beatings."

JUL. 3, 1978 First drawing by Roz Chast.

SEP. 15, 1980 This issue marks the end of metal engravings and the beginning of electronic "cold type."

APR. 1985 *The New Yorker* magazine shareholders vote to sell the magazine to Advance Publications.

MAR. 2, 1987 First issue edited by Robert Gottlieb, after the retirement of William Shawn.

APR. 18, 1988 A new size, type, and layout for the table of contents.

FEB. 20, 1989 Large illustrations and additional text first used in the Goings On section.

FEB. 20–MAR. 6, 1989 Ian Frazier's three-part Reporter at Large "Great Plains."

JUN. 29, 1992 "Career Move," the first short story by Martin Amis.

OCT. 5, 1992 First issue edited by Tina Brown.

OCT. 12, 1992 Richard Avedon's first photograph, of Malcolm X.

OCT. 26, 1992 Richard Preston's "Crisis in the Hot Zone," about the deadly Ebola virus.

DEC. 8, 1992 William Shawn dies.

1993 Françoise Mouly succeeds Lee Lorenz as art editor. Lorenz continues as cartoon editor.

MAY 17, 1993 Henry Louis Gates, Jr.,'s first fact piece, a Reflections on civil rights.

DEC. 6, 1993 Entire issue (including the cover) is devoted to Mark Danner's "The Truth of El Mozote."

FEB. 21, 1994 For the first time, the anniversary issue does not feature Irvin's Eustace Tilley on the cover; R. Crumb's "Elvis Tilley" appears instead.

MAR. 21, 1994 First full-frontal male nude appears, in a cartoon by Peter Steiner. A middle-aged man stands before his wife in a bedroom, nude, and says, accusingly, "You liked it in 'The Piano.'"

JUN. 27 & JUL. 4, 1994 First double issue, a fiction issue.

DEC. 18, 1995 Philip Gourevitch's Letter from Rwanda, about genocide during the civil war there.

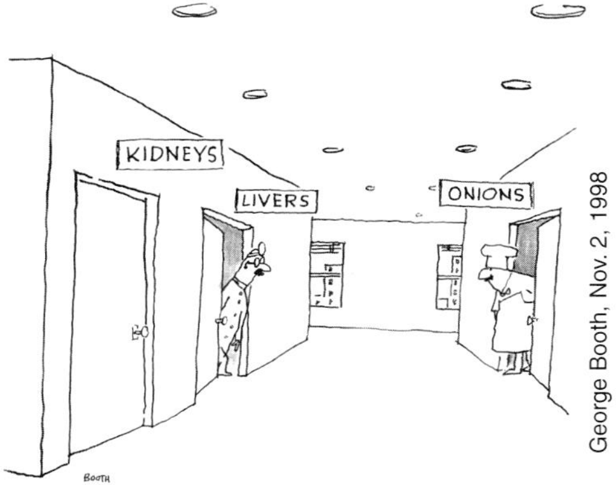

George Booth, Nov. 2, 1998

APR. 22, 1996 Steve Martin's first humor piece, "Yes in My Own Back Yard."

1997 Robert Mankoff succeeds Lee Lorenz as cartoon editor.

Victoria Roberts, Jun. 5, 2000

"Good news, honey—seventy is the new fifty."

MAY 26, 1997 Beginning with this issue, bylines appear regularly in the Talk of the Town section.

SEPT. 22, 1997 For the first time, the magazine runs biographical notes for contributors.

AUG. 3, 1998 David Remnick's first issue as editor.

FEB. 21 & 28, 2000 75th Anniversary issue cover features a photo of William Wegman's weimaraner, posing as Eustace Tilley. At 300 pages, it is the biggest issue in the history of the magazine.

ABOUT THE ARTISTS

Total number of covers for living artists is as of the July 3, 2000, issue.

CHARLES ADDAMS
Born 1912, Westfield, New Jersey
Died 1988, New York City
First *New Yorker* cover: January 1, 1938
Last *New Yorker* cover: October 30, 1989 (the Halloween issue)
Total number of *New Yorker* covers: 64
Selected books: *Drawn and Quartered* (1942); *Addams and Evil* (1947); *Monster Rally* (1950); *Homebodies* (1954); *Nightcrawlers* (1957); *Black Maria* (1960); *The Groaning Board* (1964); *My Crowd* (1970); *Favorite Haunts* (1976); *Creature Comforts* (1981); *The World of Chas Addams* (1991)

CONSTANTIN ALAJÁLOV
Born 1900, Rostov-on-Don, Russia
Died 1987, Amenia, New York
First *New Yorker* cover: September 25, 1926
Last *New Yorker* cover: September 24, 1960
Total number of *New Yorker* covers: 170
Selected books: *Conversation Pieces* (commentary by Janet Flanner; 1942); *That's Me All Over* (by Cornelia Otis Skinner; 1948); *Nuts in May* (by Cornelia Otis Skinner; 1950)

PETER ARNO
Born 1904, New York City
Died 1968, Port Chester, New York
First *New Yorker* cover: November 27, 1926
Last *New Yorker* cover: June 15, 1968
Total number of *New Yorker* covers: 99
Selected books: *Peter Arno's Cartoon Revue* (1941); *Man in the Shower* (1944); *Sizzling Platter* (1949); *Ladies & Gentlemen* (1951); *Hell of a Way to Run a Railroad* (1956); *Lady in the Shower* (1967); *Peter Arno* (1979)

ISTVAN BANYAI
Born 1949, Budapest, Hungary
Lives in New York City
First *New Yorker* cover: April 20, 1998
Total number of *New Yorker* covers: 1
Selected books: *Zoom* (1995); *Re-Zoom* (1995); *REM: Rapid Eye Movement* (1997)

ABE BIRNBAUM
Born 1899, New York City
Died 1966, New York City
First *New Yorker* cover: May 20, 1944
Last *New Yorker* cover: May 27, 1974
Total number of *New Yorker* covers: 141
Selected books: *Green Eyes* (1954); *Did a Bear Just Walk There?* (by Ann Rand; 1966)

R.O. BLECHMAN
Born 1930, Brooklyn, New York
Lives in New York City
First *New Yorker* cover: April 29, 1974
Total number of *New Yorker* covers: 14
Selected books: *R.O. Blechman: Behind the Lines* (1980); *The Life of Saint Nicholas* (1996); *The Book of Jonah* (1997)

HARRY BLISS
Born 1964, Rochester, New York
Lives in Burlington, Vermont
First *New Yorker* cover: January 5, 1998
Total number of *New Yorker* covers: 10

BARRY BLITT
Born 1958, Montreal, Canada
Lives in Greenwich, Connecticut
First *New Yorker* cover: January 10, 1994
Total number of *New Yorker* covers: 16
Selected books: *Political Babble: The 1,000 Dumbest Things Ever Said by Politicians* (by David Olive; 1992)

VLADIMIR BOBRITSKY
Born 1898, Ukraine, Russia
Died 1986, Ulster, New York
First *New Yorker* cover: February 6, 1926
Last *New Yorker* cover: May 28, 1938
Total number of *New Yorker* covers: 7

GEORGE BOOTH
Born 1926, Cainesville, Missouri
Lives in Long Island, New York
First *New Yorker* cover: November 26, 1973
Total number of *New Yorker* covers: 16
Selected books: *Think Good Thoughts About a Pussycat* (1975); *Rehearsal's Off!* (1976); *Pussycats Need Love, Too* (1980); *Omnibooth* (edited and designed by Kenneth R. Hine; 1984); *Booth Again!* (1989); *The Essential George Booth* (compiled and edited by Lee Lorenz; 1998)

JULIETTE BORDA
Born 1967, Philadelphia, Pennsylvania
Lives in New York City
First *New Yorker* cover: September 7, 1998
Total number of *New Yorker* covers: 1

STEVE BRODNER
Born 1954, Brooklyn, New York
Lives in New York City
First *New Yorker* cover: November 29, 1999
Total number of *New Yorker* covers: 1
Selected books: *Fold 'n' Tuck* (1990); *Davy Crockett* (by James Howard Kunstler; 1995); *Sharing the Pie: A Citizen's Guide to Wealth and Power* (by Steve Brouwer; 1998)

CHARLES BURNS
Born 1955, Washington, D.C.
Lives in Philadelphia, Pennsylvania
First *New Yorker* cover: November 1, 1993
Total number of *New Yorker* covers: 2
Selected books: *El Borbah* (1999); *Skin Deep: Tales of Doomed Romance* (2000); *Big Baby* (2000)

CEESEPE
Born 1958, Madrid, Spain
Lives in Madrid, Spain
First *New Yorker* cover: November 22, 1993
Total number of *New Yorker* covers: 1
Selected books: *Dibujos (Drawings)* (1982); *Barcelona by Night* (1982); *Paris-Madrid* (1985); *El Dificil Arte de la Mentira (The Difficult Art of Telling Lies)* (1986); *Libro Blanco (White Book)* (1990); *Arts Morundi* (1990)

ROZ CHAST
Born 1954, Brooklyn, New York
Lives in Connecticut
First *New Yorker* cover: August 4, 1986
Total number of *New Yorker* covers: 6
Selected books: *Unscientific Americans* (1982); *Childproof: Cartoons About Parents and Children* (1997); *Rationalizations to Live By* (by Henry Beard, Andy Borowitz, and John Boswell; 2000)

SUE COE
Born 1951, Tamworth, England
Lives in New York City
First *New Yorker* cover: March 15, 1993
Total number of *New Yorker* covers: 1
Selected books: *How to Commit Suicide in South Africa* (1983); *Paintings and Drawings* (1985); *Dead Meat* (1995); *Pit's Letter* (2000)

RAÚL COLÓN
Born 1952, New York City
Lives in New City, New York
First *New Yorker* cover: March 27, 2000
Total number of *New Yorker* covers: 1
Selected books: *My Mama Had a Dancing Heart* (by Libba Moore Gray; 1995); *A Weave of Words: An Armenian Tale* (retold by Robert D. San Souci; 1998); *Hercules* (by Robert Burleigh; 1999); *Secrets from the Dollhouse* (by Ann Turner; 2000)

WILL COTTON
Born 1882, Newport, Rhode Island
Died 1958, Stockton, New Jersey
First *New Yorker* cover: November 5, 1932
Last *New Yorker* cover: December 22, 1951
Total number of *New Yorker* covers: 55
Selected books: *The Spy* (by James Fenimore Cooper; 1929); *The Three Wayfarers; A Play in One Act* (by Thomas Hardy; 1930)

R. CRUMB
Born 1943, Philadelphia, Pennsylvania
Lives in the South of France
First *New Yorker* cover: February 21, 1994
Total number of *New Yorker* covers: 1
Selected books: *The Complete Crumb* (edited by Gary Groth with Robert Fiore; 1987); *R. Crumb's America* (1995); *The R. Crumb Coffee Table Art Book* (edited and designed by Peter Poplaski; 1997)

DANUTA DABROWSKA-SIEMASZKIEWICZ
Born 1951, Stary Sacz, Poland
Lives in Kraków, Poland
First *New Yorker* cover: November 8, 1999
Total number of *New Yorker* covers: 1

JAMES H. DAUGHERTY (JIMMIE THE INK)
Born 1889, Asheville, North Carolina
Died 1974, Boston, Massachusetts
First *New Yorker* cover: September 5, 1925
Last *New Yorker* cover: January 23, 1926
Total number of *New Yorker* covers: 2
Selected books: *Andy and the Lion: A Tale of Kindness Remembered, or the Power of Gratitude* (1938); *Poor Richard* (1941); *The Magna Charta* (1956)

ROBERT J. DAY
Born 1901, San Bernardino, California
Died 1985, St. Louis, Missouri
First *New Yorker* cover: November 4, 1933
Last *New Yorker* cover: November 24, 1956
Total number of *New Yorker* covers: 8
Selected books: *All Out for the Sack Race!* (1945);

Stories I Like to Tell (by Arthur Godfrey; 1952); *Rome Wasn't Burned in a Day* (by Leo Rosten; 1972)

JACQUES DE LOUSTAL
Born 1956, Neuilly-sur-Seine, France
Lives in Paris, France
First *New Yorker* cover: October 11, 1993
Total number of *New Yorker* covers: 3
Selected books: *Barney and the Blue Note* (with Philip Paringaux; 1987); *Kid Congo* (with Philip Paringaux; 1997); *White Sonya* (with Jerome Charyn; 2000)

PETER DE SÈVE
Born 1958, Queens, New York
Lives in Brooklyn, New York
First *New Yorker* cover: September 6, 1993
Total number of *New Yorker* covers: 12
Selected books: *Finn McCoul* (by Brian Gleeson; 1995)

LEONARD DOVE
Born c. 1907
Died 1972, New York City
First *New Yorker* cover: May 5, 1928
Last *New Yorker* cover: August 20, 1960
Total number of *New Yorker* covers: 57

ERIC DROOKER
Born 1958, New York City
Lives in San Francisco
First *New Yorker* cover: September 12, 1994
Total number of *New Yorker* covers: 6
Selected books: *FLOOD!: A Novel in Pictures* (1992); *Illuminated Poems* (by Allen Ginsberg; 1996); *Street Posters & Ballads* (1998)

IAN FALCONER
Born 1959, Ridgefield, Connecticut
Lives in New York City
First *New Yorker* cover: July 8, 1996
Total number of *New Yorker* covers: 13
Selected books: *Olivia* (2000)

FLOC'H
Born 1953, Mayenne, France
Lives in Paris, France
First *New Yorker* cover: February 10, 1997
Total number of *New Yorker* covers: 1
Selected books: *Journal d'un New-Yorkais* (by Michel Jourde; 1994)

ARTHUR GETZ
Born 1913, Passaic, New Jersey
Died 1996, Sharon, Connecticut
First *New Yorker* cover: July 23, 1938
Last *New Yorker* cover: August 29, 1988
Total number of *New Yorker* covers: 210
Selected books: *Tar Beach* (1979); *Humphrey, the Dancing Pig* (1980)

CARTER GOODRICH
Born 1959, Washington, D.C.
Lives in Los Angeles, California
First *New Yorker* cover: December 19, 1994
Total number of *New Yorker* covers: 6
Selected books: *A Christmas Carol* (by Charles Dickens; 1996)

HA (*see* Bob Zoell)

TOM HACHTMAN
Born 1948, Rockville Center, New York
Lives in Point Pleasant Beach, New Jersey
First *New Yorker* cover: August 8, 1994
Total number of *New Yorker* covers: 1
Selected books: *Gertrude's Follies* (1980); *Tom Hachtman's DoubleTakes* (1984)

THEODORE G. HAUPT
Born 1902, New York City
Died 1990, Marion, Indiana
First *New Yorker* cover: September 3, 1927
Last *New Yorker* cover: January 21, 1933
Total number of *New Yorker* covers: 44

HELEN E. HOKINSON
Born 1893, Mendota, Illinois
Died 1949, en route by air to Washington, D.C.
First *New Yorker* cover: July 16, 1927
Last *New Yorker* cover: June 23, 1951
Total number of *New Yorker* covers: 68
Selected books: *So You're Going to Buy a Book!* (1931); *My Best Girls* (1941); *When Were You Built?* (1948); *The Ladies, God Bless 'Em!* (1950); *There Are Ladies Present* (1952); *The Hokinson Festival* (1956)

REA IRVIN
Born 1881, San Francisco, California
Died 1972, St. Croix, U.S. Virgin Islands
First *New Yorker* cover: February 21, 1925 (Eustace Tilley)
Last *New Yorker* cover: July 12, 1958
Total number of *New Yorker* covers: 169
Selected books: *Crosby Gaige's Cocktail Guide and Ladies' Companion* (1941); *Snoot If You Must* (by Lucius Beebe; 1943)

JIMMIE THE INK (*see* James H. Daugherty)

WILLIAM JOYCE
Born 1957, Shreveport, Louisiana
Lives in Shreveport, Louisiana
First *New Yorker* cover: April 4, 1994
Total number of *New Yorker* covers: 8
Selected books: *Dinosaur Bob* (1988); *Santa Calls* (1993); *The Leaf Men and the Brave Good Bugs* (1996); *Rolie Polie Olie* (1999)

ANA JUAN
Born 1961, Valencia, Spain
Lives in Madrid, Spain
First *New Yorker* cover: October 16, 1995
Total number of *New Yorker* covers: 3
Selected books: *La Luna Ayuda* (1988); *Ciencias Naturales* (1989); *A Red Wind* (1992); *Lovers* (2000)

MAIRA KALMAN
Born 1949, Tel Aviv, Israel
Lives in New York City
First *New Yorker* cover: December 4, 1995
Total number of *New Yorker* covers: 5
Selected books: *Hey Willy, See the Pyramids* (1988); *Ooh-la-la (Max in Love)* (1991); *Next Stop, Grand Central* (1999); *(un)FASHION* (with Tibor Kalman; 2000)

ILONKA KARASZ
Born 1896, Budapest, Hungary
Died 1981, Brewster, New York
First *New Yorker* cover: April 4, 1925
Last *New Yorker* cover: October 22, 1973
Total number of *New Yorker* covers: 186

CHIP KIDD
Born 1964, Reading, Pennsylvania
Lives in New York City
First *New Yorker* cover: June 21 & 28, 1999
Total number of *New Yorker* covers: 1
Selected books: *Batman Collected* (1996); *Batman Animated* (1998)

CLAYTON KNIGHT
Born 1891
Died 1969
First *New Yorker* cover: April 17, 1926
Last *New Yorker* cover: April 17, 1926
Total number of *New Yorker* covers: 1

VITALY KOMAR
Born 1943, Moscow, U.S.S.R.
Lives in New York City
First *New Yorker* cover: July 12, 1993
Total number of *New Yorker* covers: 1
Selected books: *Komar/Melamid, Two Soviet Dissident Artists* (with Alexander Melamid, edited by Melvyn B. Nathanson; 1978); *Komar & Melamid* (1988); *Painting by Numbers: Komar & Melamid's Scientific Guide to Art* (with Alexander Melamid, edited by JoAnn Wypijewski; 1997)

EDWARD KOREN
Born 1935, New York City
Lives in Brookfield, Vermont
First *New Yorker* cover: August 28, 1971
Total number of *New Yorker* covers: 24
Selected books: *What About Me?* (1989); *Quality Time: Parenting, Progeny, and Pets* (1995); *The Hard Work of Simple Living: A Somewhat Blank Book for the Sustainable Hedonist* (1998)

ADOLPH K. KRONENGOLD
Born 1900, New Orleans, Louisiana
Died 1986, New Orleans, Louisiana
First *New Yorker* cover: September 22, 1928
Last *New Yorker* cover: January 18, 1947
Total number of *New Yorker* covers: 22

ANITA KUNZ
Born 1956, Toronto, Canada
Lives in Toronto and New York City
First *New Yorker* cover: July 10, 1995
Total number of *New Yorker* covers: 2

PIERRE LE-TAN
Born 1950, Paris, France
Lives in Paris, France
First *New Yorker* cover: February 14, 1970
Total number of *New Yorker* covers: 18
Selected books: *Remarkable Names* (by John Train; 1977); *Album* (1990); *Cleo's Christmas Dreams* (1995)

MARISCAL
Born 1950, Valencia, Spain
Lives in Barcelona, Spain
First *New Yorker* cover: August 9, 1993
Total number of *New Yorker* covers: 5
Selected books: *Javier Mariscal: Designing the New Spain* (by Emma Dent Coad; 1991); *Señor Mundo and Me: A Happy Birthday Story* (by Kim Summers; 1998)

Charles E. Martin
Born 1910, Boston, Massachusetts
Died 1995, Portland, Maine
First *New Yorker* cover: August 6, 1938
Last *New Yorker* cover: February 9, 1987
Total number of *New Yorker* covers: 185
Selected books: *Big Orange Thing* (by Jerry Juhl; 1969); *Noah's Ark* (retold by Lawrence T. Lorimer; 1978); *Island Winter* (1984); *Island Rescue* (1985)

Franco Matticchio
Born 1957, Varese, Italy
Lives in Varese, Italy
First *New Yorker* cover: December 13, 1999
Total number of *New Yorker* covers: 1
Selected books: *Sensa Senso* (1994); *Sogni e Disegni* (1997)

Lorenzo Mattotti
Born 1954, Brescia, Italy
Lives in Paris, France
First *New Yorker* cover: June 21, 1993
Total number of *New Yorker* covers: 11
Selected books: *Fires* (1988); *Eugenio* (by Marianne Cockenpot; 1993); *Murmur* (by Jerry Kramsky; 1993); *Pinocchio* (by Carlo Collodi; 1993)

Max
Born 1956, Barcelona, Spain
Lives in Mallorca, Spain
First *New Yorker* cover: December 18, 1995
Total number of *New Yorker* covers: 2
Selected books: *The Extended Dream of Mr. D* (1998)

David Mazzucchelli
Born 1960, Providence, Rhode Island
Lives in New York City
First *New Yorker* cover: July 26, 1993
Total number of *New Yorker* covers: 3
Selected books: *Batman: Year One* (with Frank Miller; 1988); *Paul Auster's City of Glass* (with Paul Karasik; 1994); *La Géométrie de l'Obsession* (1997)

Bruce McCall
Born 1935, Simcoe, Ontario
Lives in New York City
First *New Yorker* cover: August 16, 1993
Total number of *New Yorker* covers: 14
Selected books: *Zany Afternoons* (1982); *Thin Ice: Coming of Age in Canada* (1997)

Richard McGuire
Born 1957, Perth Amboy, New Jersey
Lives in New York City
First *New Yorker* cover: December 27, 1993
Total number of *New Yorker* covers: 5
Selected books: *The Orange Book* (1994); *What Goes Around Comes Around* (1995); *What's Wrong with This Book?* (1997)

Alexander Melamid
Born 1945, Moscow, U.S.S.R.
Lives in Jersey City, New Jersey
First *New Yorker* cover: July 12, 1993
Total number of *New Yorker* covers: 1
Selected books: *Komar/Melamid, Two Soviet Dissident Artists* (with Vitaly Komar, edited by Melvyn B. Nathanson; 1978); *Komar & Melamid* (1988); *Painting by Numbers: Komar and Melamid's Scientific Guide to Art* (with Vitaly Komar, edited by JoAnn Wypijewski; 1997)

Richard Merkin
Born 1938, Brooklyn, New York
Lives in New York City
First *New Yorker* cover: April 5, 1993
Total number of *New Yorker* covers: 3
Selected books: *Leagues Apart: The Men and Times of the Negro Baseball Leagues* (by Lawrence S. Ritter; 1995); *Tijuana Bibles* (by Bob Adelman; 1997)

Ever Meulen
Born 1946, Kuurne, Belgium
Lives in Brussels, Belgium
First *New Yorker* cover: May 23, 1994
Total number of *New Yorker* covers: 3

M. Scott Miller
Born 1969, Missoula, Montana
Lives in Brooklyn, New York
First *New Yorker* cover: June 3, 1996
Total number of *New Yorker* covers: 3

Roxie Munro
Born 1945, Mineral Wells, Texas
Lives in New York City
First *New Yorker* cover: November 9, 1981
Total number of *New Yorker* covers: 14
Selected books: *The Inside-Outside Book of New York City* (1985); *Architects Make Zigzags: Looking at Architecture from A to Z* (1986); *The Inside-Outside Book of Libraries* (by Julie Cummins; 1996); *Crocodiles, Camels & Dugout Canoes: Eight Adventurous Episodes* (by Bo Zaunders; 1998)

R. Kenton Nelson
Born 1954, Los Angeles, California
Lives in Pasadena, California
First *New Yorker* cover: April 26 & May 3, 1999
Total number of *New Yorker* covers: 2
Selected books: *Picturing a Perfect World: The Paintings of R. Kenton Nelson* (1998)

Kathy Osborn
Born 1955, Rochester, New York
Lives in Brooklyn, New York
First *New Yorker* cover: October 17, 1988
Total number of *New Yorker* covers: 17
Selected books: *The Joke's on George* (by Michael O. Tunnell; 1993); *The Emperor's Garden* (by Ferida Wolff; 1994); *I Forgot My Shoes* (by Jessica Harper; 1999)

Mary Petty
Born 1899, Hampton, New Jersey
Died 1976, Paramus, New Jersey
First *New Yorker* cover: June 29, 1940
Last *New Yorker* cover: March 19, 1966
Total number of *New Yorker* covers: 38
Selected books: *Good-Bye, Mr. Chippendale* (by Terence Harold Robsjohn-Gibbings; 1944); *This Petty Pace* (1945)

George Price
Born 1901, Coytesville, New Jersey
Died 1995, Englewood, New Jersey
First *New Yorker* cover: Dec. 25, 1965
Last *New Yorker* cover: Dec. 25, 1965
Total number of *New Yorker* covers: 1
Selected books: *Good Humor Man* (1940); *It's Smart to Be People* (1942); *Who's in Charge Here?* (1944); *Cartoons by George Price* (1944); *Is It Anyone We Know?* (1944); *Ice Cold War* (1951); *We Buy Old Gold* (1951); *George Price's Characters* (1955); *My Dear 500 Friends* (1963); *Browse at Your Own Risk* (1977); *The World of George Price* (1987)

Max Rée
First *New Yorker* cover: September 19, 1925
Last *New Yorker* cover: December 5, 1925
Total number of *New Yorker* covers: 4

George Riemann
Born 1961, Seesen, West Germany
Lives in San Francisco, California
First *New Yorker* cover: February 6, 1995
Total number of *New Yorker* covers: 3

Robert Risko
Born 1956, Ellwood City, Pennsylvania
Lives in New York City
First *New Yorker* cover: November 2, 1992
Total number of *New Yorker* covers: 3
Selected books: *The Risko Book* (2000)

Michael Roberts
Born 1947, London, England
Lives in Paris, France
First *New Yorker* cover: April 29 & May 6, 1996
Total number of *New Yorker* covers: 17
Selected books: *The Jungle ABC* (1998); *Mumbo Jumbo* (2000)

Denis Roche
Born 1967, New Haven, Connecticut
Lives in Providence, Rhode Island
First *New Yorker* cover: August 18, 1997
Total number of *New Yorker* covers: 1
Selected books: *Ollie All Over* (1997); *Art Around the World!: Loo-Loo, Boo and More Art You Can Do* (1998); *The Teeny Tiny Teacher* (by Stephanie Calmenson; 1998)

Dean Rohrer
Born 1953, Harrisonburg, Virginia
Lives in Marlton, New Jersey
First *New Yorker* cover: February 8, 1999
Total number of *New Yorker* covers: 1

Arnold Roth
Born 1929, Philadelphia, Pennsylvania
Lives in New York City
First *New Yorker* cover: November 16, 1992
Total number of *New Yorker* covers: 4
Selected books: *A Sports Bestiary* (by George Plimpton; 1982); *No Pain, No Strain: Further Uses for Exercise Equipment* (1996); *Poor Arnold's Almanac* (1998); *The Lexicon* (by William F. Buckley, Jr.; 1998)

David Sandlin
Born 1956, Belfast, Northern Ireland
Lives in New York City
First *New Yorker* cover: January 22, 1996
Total number of *New Yorker* covers: 1
Selected books: *Land of 1000 Beers: La Via Dollarosa* (1989)

Charles Saxon
Born 1920, New York City
Died 1988, New Canaan, Connecticut
First *New Yorker* cover: December 19, 1959
Last *New Yorker* cover: September 26, 1988
Total number of *New Yorker* covers: 92
Selected books: *Oh, Happy, Happy, Happy!* (1960); *One Man's Fancy* (1977); *"Honesty Is One of the Better Policies": Saxon's World of Business* (1984)

J. OTTO SEIBOLD
Born 1960, Oakland, California
Lives in San Francisco, California
First *New Yorker* cover: December 6, 1999
Total number of *New Yorker* covers: 1
Selected books: *Mr. Lunch Borrows a Canoe* (with Vivian Walsh; 1994); *Free Lunch* (with Vivian Walsh; 1996); *Penguin Dreams* (with Vivian Walsh; 1999)

J.J. SEMPÉ
Born 1932, Bordeaux, France
Lives in Paris, France
First *New Yorker* cover: August 14, 1978
Total number of *New Yorker* covers: 67
Selected books: *Rien N'est Simple* (1962); *The Musicians* (1980); *Par Avion* (1991)

BARBARA SHERMUND
Born c. 1910
Died 1978
First *New Yorker* cover: October 3, 1925
Last *New Yorker* cover: August 5, 1944
Total number of *New Yorker* covers: 9

R. SIKORYAK
Born 1964, Somerville, New Jersey
Lives in New York City
First *New Yorker* cover: September 25, 1995
Total number of *New Yorker* covers: 7
Selected books: *The Seduction of Mike* (co-written by Michael Smith; 1997); *The Narrative Corpse* (editor, with Art Spiegelman; 1998)

ROSE SILVER
Born 1902, New York City
Died 1995, New York City
First *New Yorker* cover: April 13, 1929
Last *New Yorker* cover: January 30, 1932
Total number of *New Yorker* covers: 7

GRETCHEN DOW SIMPSON
Born 1939, Cambridge, Massachusetts
Lives in Providence, Rhode Island
First *New Yorker* cover: August 19, 1974
Total number of *New Yorker* covers: 58
Selected books: *Gretchen's ABC* (1991)

OWEN SMITH
Born 1964, Fremont, California
Lives in Alameda, California
First *New Yorker* cover: December 6, 1993
Total number of *New Yorker* covers: 10
Selected books: *The Jack Tales* (stories by Ray Hicks as told to Lynn Salsi; 2000)

WINSTON SMITH
Born 1952, Oklahoma City, Oklahoma
Lives in San Francisco, California
First *New Yorker* cover: August 23 & 30, 1999
Total number of *New Yorker* covers: 2
Selected books: *Act Like Nothing's Wrong: The Montage Art of Winston Smith* (1994); *Artcrime: The Montage Art of Winston Smith, Volume 2* (1999)

EDWARD SOREL
Born 1929, Bronx, New York
Lives in New York City
First *New Yorker* cover: October 5, 1992
Total number of *New Yorker* covers: 36
Selected books: *First Encounters: A Book of Memorable Meetings* (with Nancy Caldwell Sorel; 1994); *Unauthorized Portraits* (1997); *The Saturday Kid* (with Cheryl Carlesimo; 2000)

ART SPIEGELMAN
Born 1948, Stockholm, Sweden
Lives in New York City
First *New Yorker* cover: February 15, 1993
Total number of *New Yorker* covers: 29
Selected books: *RAW* magazine (editor, with Françoise Mouly; 1980-1991); *The Wild Party: The Lost Classic* (by Joseph Moncure March; 1994); *Open Me... I'm a Dog!* (1997); *Maus: A Survivor's Tale* (1997); *The Narrative Corpse* (editor, with R. Sikoryak; 1998); *Comix, Essays, Graphics and Scraps* (1998); *Little Lit: Folklore & Fairy Tale Funnies* (editor, with Françoise Mouly; 2000)

WILLIAM STEIG
Born 1907, New York City
Lives in Boston, Massachusetts
First *New Yorker* cover: May 7, 1932
Total number of *New Yorker* covers: 120
Selected books: *William Steig Drawings* (1979); *Doctor De Soto* (1982); *Ruminations* (1984); *Strutters & Fretters; or, The Inescapable Self* (1992); *The World of William Steig* (edited by Lee Lorenz; 1998)

SAUL STEINBERG
Born 1914, Ramnicul-Sarat, Romania
Died 1999, New York City
First *New Yorker* cover: January 13, 1945
Last *New Yorker* cover: August 16, 1999
Total number of *New Yorker* covers: 87
Selected books: *All in Line* (1945); *This Is the Story* (by David L. Cohn; 1947); *The Art of Living* (1949); *The Passport* (1954); *The Labyrinth* (1960); *The New World* (1965); *The Inspector* (1973); *Saul Steinberg* (1978); *Saul Steinberg: The Discovery of America* (1992)

JAMES STEVENSON
Born 1929, New York City
Lives in Guilford, Connecticut
First *New Yorker* cover: January 6, 1962
Total number of *New Yorker* covers: 78
Selected books: *Sorry Lady, This Beach Is Private!* (1963); *Something Marvelous Is About to Happen* (1971); *Let's Boogie!* (1978); *Uptown Local, Downtown Express* (1983)

JOOST SWARTE
Born 1947, Heemstede, The Netherlands
Lives in Haarlem, The Netherlands
First *New Yorker* cover: October 5, 1998
Total number of *New Yorker* covers: 1
Selected books: *Joost Swarte's Modern Art* (1980); *Swarte, hors Série* (1984); *Glas en Lood* (1999)

RICHARD TAYLOR
Born 1902, Fort William, Ontario
Died 1970, Bethel, Connecticut
First *New Yorker* cover: January 9, 1937
Last *New Yorker* cover: January 31, 1942
Total number of *New Yorker* covers: 4
Selected books: *The Better Taylors* (1944); *Introduction to Cartooning* (1947); *Butchered Baseball* (by F. S. Pearson 2d; 1952); *R. Taylor's Wrong Bag* (1961)

JAMES THURBER
Born 1894, Columbus, Ohio
Died 1961, New York City
First *New Yorker* cover: January 29, 1936
Last *New Yorker* cover: January 9, 1946
Total number of *New Yorker* covers: 6
Selected books: *The Seal in the Bedroom & Other Predicaments* (1932); *Fables for Our Time and Famous Poems* (1940); *Thurber's Men, Women, and Dogs* (1943); *The Beast in Me and Other Animals* (1948); *The Wonderful O* (1957); *Thurber & Co.* (1966)

SAN TOYO
First *New Yorker* cover: April 2, 1927
Last *New Yorker* cover: April 2, 1927
Total number of *New Yorker* covers: 1

MARK ULRIKSEN
Born 1957, San Francisco, California
Lives in San Francisco, California
First *New Yorker* cover: May 30, 1994
Total number of *New Yorker* covers: 14

BENOÎT VAN INNIS
Born 1960, Brugge, Belgium
Lives in Brussels, Belgium
First *New Yorker* cover: February 5, 1990
Total number of *New Yorker* covers: 14
Selected books: *Le Musée Interdit* (1990); *Oncle Gilbert* (1995); *Bravo! Bravo!* (2000)

CHRIS WARE
Born 1967, Omaha, Nebraska
Lives in Chicago, Illinois
First *New Yorker* cover: June 21 & 28, 1999
Total number of *New Yorker* covers: 1
Selected books: *Jimmy Corrigan: The Smartest Kid on Earth* (2000)

WILLIAM WEGMAN
Born 1943, Holyoke, Massachusetts
Lives in New York City
First *New Yorker* cover: February 21 & 28, 2000
Total number of *New Yorker* covers: 1
Selected books: *Fay* (1999); *Surprise Party* (2000); *William Wegman: Fashion Photographs* (2000); *William Wegman's The Night Before Christmas* (2000)

MICHAEL WITTE
Born 1944, St. Louis, Missouri
Lives in South Nyack, New York
First *New Yorker* cover: February 11, 1980
Total number of *New Yorker* covers: 2
Selected books: *The Book of Terms* (with Peter Delacorte; 1978); *Otter Nonsense* (by Norton Juster; 1994)

MARK ZINGARELLI
Born 1952, Pittsburgh, Pennsylvania
Lives in Irwin, Pennsylvania
First *New Yorker* cover: June 6, 1994
Total number of *New Yorker* covers: 1

BOB ZOELL (HA)
Born 1940, Regina, Saskatchewan
Lives in Los Angeles, California
First *New Yorker* cover: June 20, 1994
Total number of *New Yorker* covers: 4
Selected books: *Air Powered: The Art of the Airbrush* (with Rick Probst and W. Scott Griffiths; 1979)

INDEX OF ILLUSTRATIONS

On the following pages are six detachable ready-to-frame prints.

Jan. 24, 1994
THE NEW YORKER
Price $2.50

overleaf:

TAILED
by Peter de Sève
January 24, 1994

Price $3.00

THE NEW YORKER

May 31, 1999

overleaf:

LOST TIMES SQUARE
by Bruce McCall
May 31, 1999

May 3, 1993
THE NEW YORKER
Price $1.95
2A
sempé.

overleaf:

BALLET'S NEW SPRING
by J.J. Sempé
May 3, 1993

Feb. 24 & Mar. 3, 1997
THE NEW YORKER
Price $3.50
art spiegelman
CRIME
AND
PUNISHMENT

overleaf:

DICK TILLEY

by Art Spiegelman

February 24 & March 3, 1997

Oct. 4, 1993

THE

NEW YORKER

Price $1.95

overleaf:

REMEMBRANCE OF FLINGS PAST
by Edward Sorel
October 4, 1993

Feb. 13, 1995
THE NEW YORKER
Price $2.50
LEXINGTON AVE
WILSHIRE
BLVD
ST
IRT

overleaf:

WILSHIRE & LEX
by Saul Steinberg
February 13, 1995

From COVERING THE NEW YORKER, *published by Abbeville Press.*